SOCIAL CHANGE IN INDIA

Social Change in India Crisis and Resilience

Yogendra Singh

HAR-ANAND
PUBLICATIONS PVT LTD

Reprint, 2025

Published by Ashok Gosain and Ashish Gosain for:
HAR-ANAND PUBLICATIONS PVT LTD
E-49/3, Okhla Industrial Area, Phase-II, New Delhi-110020
Tel: 41603490
E-mail: info@haranandbooks.com/haranand@rediffmail.com
Shop online at: www.haranandbooks.com

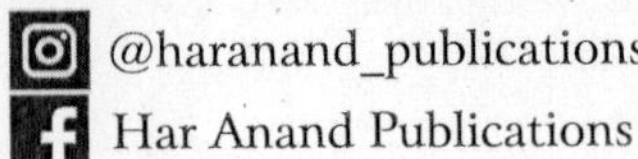

Printed in India

FOR GUJRATI DEVI

Preface

The essays in the volume were written for seminars, conferences and academic gatherings spanning a decade. Many of them have been published in collections of proceedings of seminars, and a few were published in journals. The institutions and academic bodies whom the author would like to acknowledge are the ICSSR, New Delhi; the Indian Academy of Social Sciences, Allahabad; the Centre for Development Studies, Surat; the Christian Academy, Seoul (South Korea); Centre for the Study of Social systems, JNU; and Man and Development (Chandigarh). The paper on "Law and Social Change in India" was presented at an Indo-American colloquium at the Fletcher Law Institute at Harvard University. The chapter on "Ethnicity, Unity and Indian vicilization", is based on a paper presented at a seminar on the theme of Indian Revolution held in Leningrad (not Petrograd) under the joint Indo-Soviet auspices.

I have benefited from several constructive suggestions and comments from scholars in India and abroad. To all of them I remain grateful. Shri Hulas Singh has helped in editorial improvement of the text with meticulous care. Shri Narendra Kumar has taken keen interest in prodding me to complete the volume for publication on time. I remain grateful to both of them. There may still remain flaws in the presentation of ideas or in the composition of the text. The responsibility for this is mine alone.

Yogendra Singh

Contents

Chapter I

Introduction

To comprehend the process of social change in India, to put together the diverse factors, cultural, social, economic and political, etc. into a manageable configuration in order to explain the patterns of change has always posed difficulties. But today this task is further made complex as the ideologies or the paradigms defining the normative direction of social change have assumed numerous contradictory orientations. Moreover, the skewed pattern of social mobility, the narrow cultural self-consciousness among tribes, castes, religious minorities and interest groups and the cumulative result of the socialization of people into a political culture increasingly losing legitimation have introduced elements that render outcome of social change unpredictable. Nevertheless, one may attempt to understand the process of social change in India as a response to a set of key challenges to the evolution of this society into a democrtic nation state anchored on principles that ensure a quality of life for its citizens optimising the levels of social justice, provide secure economic life, peaceful relationships among diverse religious and ethnic groups with the inter-cultural ties leading to integrated development. It could mean better economic, educational and social opportunities for the people to articulate their citizenship rights and perform their duties.

How far have we reached nearer these goals in the course of the past forty five years of our endeavour towards social, political and economic development? Are the forces of change such that strengthen India's emergence as a nation state? Or threaten its evolution due to uneven or contradictory outcomes of the process of social change? What is the nature of such crisis? Does Indian society, its institutional structure and past tradition inhere a vitality that could provide a social resilience to overcome the forces of disintegration, crisis and obstacle to integrated social change? In this context how should "nation", "nationalism" and "civilization" be defined to analyse and comprehend the Indian reality of social processes?

The essays in this volume are an attempt to analyse some of these issues related to the process of social change in India. Compared to the situation obtaining just after independence when the ideological framework of social change in the country was being crystallized and a Constitution laying out its basic objectives was outlined, there are today two specific forms in which the situation has changed: first, there has taken place a substantial change in the social structure without simultaneously bringing about a structural change in the society. It results into tensions and often builds up social crisis. Secondly, there has taken place a sea-change in the subjective domain or the consciousness of the people in respect of social change.

The studies of social mobility and social stratification in our society indicate development, such as investment in education, agriculture, industry, the reservation policy for the weaker sections and employment and welfare programmes, etc. A very substantial middle class has emerged both in the rural and the urban sectors of society. With the growth in the population and the size of economy, this middle class today dominates the power structure of society. In the rural area the "green revolution" of the 1970's triggered the rise of the rich peasantry, and through the process of the expansion of industry and the services a very substantial urban middle class has also emerged. This class includes the government servants, industrial bluecollar workers in the state enterprises, the professionals engaged in legal, medical, managerial, banking, media and information related services and the commercial and industrial—entrepreneurial classes. Taken together these groups today constitute a very articulate, active and powerful segment of our society. If we add to this the active full-time political activists and their leadership, we get a very substantial (estimates vary from 150 to 250 millions) population of the "middle class" in our society. The key question, however, is as to what contribution does this new Class make towards achieving the normative goals of social change in our society—the goals of a democratic, secular, justice oriented nation state? Does the emergence of this class make a structural transformation in our society, say from a traditional-feudal to a secular-democratic or rational-liberal form of society? No doubt, this transition in the social structure of our society and its corresponding economic, cultural and political consequences have brought about many changes, some integrative such as the expansion of market and trade, information-networking and media exposure of the people, expansion of the services and strengthening of the integrative impulses selectively. But at the same time its negative character is reflected in the structural cleavages that now dominate the social composiuon Of the middle classes on the one hand and the lower classes on the other, as also in the ideological divide that exists between these two social categories.

The social composition of the middle class and its ideology, however, is such that does not in full measure harmonise with the national ideology or its normative goals of social change. Firstly, his class is largely drawn from the upper and middle castes; the lower castes, the tribes and the minorities are not represented in its composition commensurate to their population. The reservation policy has not helped the elevation of such groups to the extent expected. It has, on the one hand, created cleavages between the upper middle and the lower caste groups within the reserved categories. Evidence suggests that a few castes from amongst the reserved castes have disproportionately monoplised the opportunities. However, the lower castes, the minorities and tribes have on the other hand been increasingly alienated from the system contributing to militancy, social unrest and overall disenchantment. The middle classes, as most studies of social mobility show, tend to be idologically engrossed into a mind-set which decries values of liberalism, social justice and priciples of sharing or sacrifice. This class is increasingly taking to consumerist cultural ethos and short-run utilitarian values. In an economy of scarcities and lack of opportunities provided by the state this conflict of values and expectations generates mis-directed radicalism as also ethical and social opportunism on a large scale. Consequently, a rapid process of delegitimation of basic institutions of society has taken place.

We are, therefore, confronted with a situation of double crisis, one of success and the other of failures. Our investment so far in economic and social development has yielded results which we witness in the ascendancy of a new middle class. It offers dynamic inputs in social and economic change, represents in large measure the resilience of many traditional institutions such as the traditional occupations, joint family system and religious values. It strengthens market, trade and media institutions and provides a massive base of the skilled manpower so indispensable for economic growth. But this success is essentially flawed on account of its self-centred ideological moorings and its narrow social base. This we have called the "crisis" of our success". The "crisis of our failure" is however, much pervasive. It is marked by our failures in the field of abolition of poverty and social injustice. Since independence despite the efforts to abolish poverty, the country still has forty to thirty percent of its population below the poverty line. During the same period many east-

Asians countries have substantially reduced the population below the subsistance level. According to the World Bank the figure for the population living below the subsistence level in 1990 was 5 percent in South Korea, 15 percent in Indonesia and 10 per cent in China. An important reason for this success goes to the multi-level flow of the wealth generated in the society instead of its concentration in a narrow segment of the population such as the upper and middle classes as in India. Ironically, despite our profession of socialistic pattern of society, our policies in social and economic fields have been most detrimental to the prosperity of the weaker sections of society, such as the *dalits,* the women, the scheduled castes, scheduled tribes and the minorities. It is reflected also in the failure of our educational policy. The mass illiteracy in the forty per cent of the population still persists. It is higher still in the case of women. There is a vicious circular relationship between poverty, susceptibility to fall a victim to exploitation, proneness to health morbidity, high fertility rate and illiteracy. Education is a single most effective factor which breaks this process of vicious cumulative causation. We find that wherever educational achievements, whether within a region or a social group are higher, the indicators of economic growth as also of the quality of life are higher. The effective implementation of the programmes of welfare and social justice, such as the reservation of jobs for the Scheduled Castes, Scheduled Tribes and the backward classes have not yielded desirable results primarily due to lack of education. Our failure in the field of removal of illiteracy, and universalization of education is indeed at the root of the most facets of our "crisis of failures".

II

Emanating from the processes of change in the social structure and the contradictions generated by it, new ideological forces have emerged in our society. These ideologies relate to the concept of nation and nationalism, the concept of 'civilization' and integration of cultural traditions. A paradox about the relationship between the past tradition and the process of modernization in our society is that both adaptive and exclusivist tendencies in this relationship have emerged during the past few decades. There is substantial evidence provided by social science studies which shows that traditional institutions such as caste, joint family and religion which in the reckoning of many Western social scientists should have hindered the process of social change towards modernization, have played a role supportive of modernization in our society. Both Hinduism and Islam, considered to be traditionalistic in economic-ethical orientations, have not come in the way of positive response to economic entrepreneurship. Similarly, joint family has served as enabling institution for the promotion of economic enterprise, techno-economic innovations, generation of capital and promotion of credit and marketability of products. The traditional skills of castes, based on hereditary occupations have been very helpful both in agriculture and mercantile vocations to promote innovation and high productivity. The leadership in the green-revolution in most parts of the country has come from peasants whose traditional occupation was agriculture. Similarly, both Hindu and Muslims castes who were traditionally engaged in trade and crafts have stepped into the new role of commercial and marketing activities adopting modern institutional systems. These developments articulate the resilience of our traditions for adaptive response to the process of modernization. Such developments have provided positive reinforcement to the process of social change.

On the other hand, changes in our social structure have also resulted into the widening of the social inequalities; this together with the narrow cultural ethos of the middle classes has alienated the poorer sections of our society such as the tribes, lower backward castes. the Scheduled Castes etc. from the mainstream cultural ideology laid down in the Constitution. This has often led to the rejection of the notions of "nationalism" and "nation" from an articulate minority section of the population. Such groups place more emphasis on "ethnicity" and "ethnic identity" and their notion of a nation-state is that of a rigid cultural mosaic rather than an organic integrated system. Articulation of this viewpoint has also found support from a section of social scientists in our country and abroad. It is in this context that a debate on the notions of "nation-state", nation and nationalism assumes significance and the meaningful context to this debate is provided by the concepts of ethnicity and civilization.

We have argued through several essays included in this volume that a "mosaic viewpoint" of nation and nationalism tends not only to be highly positivistic (reification) but is static indeed. Often this viewpoint emanates from evaluation of nation-building in India from the normative standards derived from a narrow segment of the Western history. It is less sensitive to the historicity of Indian civilization and its relationship with the ideology of nation, nationalism and nation-state. We argue that the concept of nation in India has been of a cultural or civilizational rather than political nature. Civilization in India constituted an organic system consisting of plural elements derived from diverse cultural, ethnic, religious, political, technological and economic institutions of people belonging to different regions, castes, religions and ethnic stocks settled in India. There indeed existed a cultural and religious diversity but this diversity was not autarkic, rather it was blended into an organic system of basic values, styles, belief systems and techno-economic worldview. This constituted the unity of the Indian civilization encompassing diversities. The contemporary s6cial contradictions generated by the forces of social and economic development in our society have created cleavages both of ideology and social relationship. Hence the emergence of a "counter ideology" in contrast with the organic viewpoint of nation state.

We have also argued that "nation" as a concept may best be understood as a process rather than as a (reified) substantive institutional entity. As an organic system it is ever-evolving and self-integrating. At the global level we witness both the process of segmentarian and organic enlargement of the scope of nation-state. The breakdown of the USSR is an example of the first type and the emergence of the European Community an example of the second type. As there is more rapid progress in the domains of information systems, mass media and globalization of economy, the concept of nation-state would itself undergo major changes; its scope would be redefined and possibly it would subsist more as a cultural-civilizational phenomenon rather than as a political institution. The concepts of "state" and "sovereignty" would assume new meaning and significance. In this context, the worldview about nation as primarily a civilizational phenomenon in India assumes new merit.

These changes have introduced social and cultural cleavages in our society. The main reason behind these cleavages is not merely the extension of the gap between the rich and the poor or between the lower and the middle or upper-middle classes, in other words, the structural hiatus in society, which indeed has widened, but also the reinforcement of such cleavages through counter ideologies. Ideologies of ethnicity, religious fundamentalism, casteism and regionalism, etc. have spurred during the decades after independence. These developments have culminated into a new phase of the growth of 'communal' phenomenon in our society. Historically we inherited the legacy of communalism from the British policy of division on communal lines which resulted in the partition of the country. The decades after independence marked a period of conscious effort to override this phenomenon supplanting it with a national ideology which had evolved during the freedom movement, an ideology of secular democratic welfare state.

The processes of change, however, that took place as revealed by the studies on social mobility, social stratification, patterns of economic growth, process of industrialization and urbanization, etc. concretely demonstrate that these changes. have remained skewed favourable only to the better off sections of society. The changes were also uneven in respect of the relationship between social mobility and social aspiration. In most cases even when social mobility was handicapped or was very slow, the aspiration for mobility and strong consciousness about its legitimation was very high. This happened because of continued political participation, media exposure and increased politicization of the institutional systems of society. The emergence of the counter-ideologies took place as a result of this miss-match between expectations and actual realization of the goals of social mobility. The structural inconsistencies in the process of change generated cultural dissonance in society.

The role of 'relative deprivation,' in the growth of counter-ideologies in society though largely valid may yet require qualification, since it is not always the poor or the deprived who support or lead the movements based on such ideologies e.g. of caste, territory, ethnicity or religion. The role of the middle classes assumes significance. Indeed, one positive result of the investment in economy, education and infrastructures in our society since independence is the emergence of these middle classes in all segments of society, among traditionally forward as also several backward castes and tribes. The scale of this mobility has, however, been heavily tilted in favour of the forward sections, the upper castes and the traditionally dominant groups. In the operation of the counter ideologies both of communalism and ethnicity one may witness a crucial role of the new middle class climbers in society.

Interestingly, the ideological perception of the state, the notions of nationalism and its worldview are divergent among a large section of the new middle classes, be they Hindus, or Muslims. The Muslims tend to project their legitimate discontent about having been neglected by the state and its development apparatus in the fields of education.. employment, economic benefits and share in power. This indeed is an established fact as many studies have revealed. Even though there may be some initial structural or cultural factors which played a role in deflecting the process of social and economic development in the Muslim communities in India, the fact remains that the largest segment of their population remains backward. This backwardness has bred a feeling of alienation and despair often contributing to exclusivist or even fundamentalist responses. In this process, the Muslim religious or cultural elite instead of playing a modernizing role have more often tended to reinforce traditionalism.

Muslims, instead of forging a common front of all the backward and exploited sections of Indian society irrespective of religion or caste against the state policy and its processes of development which tended to be discriminatory, have increasingly taken resources to isolationism. Muslim elites, in India unlike their counterparts in Indonesia, Malaysia, or even Pakistan have maintained a very narrow ideological stance in defining the role of religion in economic, technological and educational development. This has, on the one hand, retarded the pace of development in Muslim society, and on the other gives scope to a large section of the Hindu new middle classes to misinterpret the situation, and give it a communal overtone. This misinterpretation is rampant today ranging from Muslim communities, response to population policy to their attitude to secularism and nationalism. Whenever, these formulations are tested against hard facts they fail to be validated, nevertheless the ideological obfuscation goes on.

The root of communalism in contemporary India have therefore a primarily social structural and economic base. But these are transcended to the level of ideology because of the negative role played by a large section of elite both in the Hindu and the Muslim communities. It is imperative that the situation is de-ideologised and brought to the level (the socio-economic and educational development of the backward amongst both the communities) where it belongs.

The essays in this volume have dealt with many facets of social change that our society is experiencing today. Each essay is complete in itself and can be read independently but there is also a continuity of ideas and their convergence on the theme of social structure, ideology and change.

Chapter 2

Contradictions and Challenges of Social Change

The study of contemporary social changes in the Indian society cannot be dissociated from the initial social conditions of the society. Its historical roots provide a base for its evaluation. The social and economic distortions created by colonialism, emergence of the ideology of freedom movement, its crystallisation in the form of the Indian Constitution, and the planning process for social transformation, are some of the historical factors which have set the direction and patterns of social changes in contemporary India. These historical forces and the social and political conditions generated by them define the shape of these social change processes. These are organically related to the 'model' that India adopted for social change.

The Indian 'Model' for Social Transformation

The objectives of social transformation in India as envisaged ideologically could be characterised as revolutionary in content and evolutionary in strategy or methods. There is structurally an intimate though ideologically discriminant relationship between revolution and evolution. This was realised by the leaders of Indian freedom movement. They had also envisioned how social structure, history and tradition which form the initial conditions of a society, set a limit to the strategies, goals and methods of social transformation. Gandhiji was foremost in his thinking in this regard. Jawaharlal Nehru completed this process by evolving a model for Indian path to social transformation. It recognised that revolutionary changes in institutions, social structures and values of the Indian society were essential if social change was to be brought about through democratic participation. One had also to employ non-violent means. This was essential part of the ideology Inherited from the leaders of national movement. Much debate in India has taken place on the class character of this movement and its orientations. Indeed, the model of social transformation that India gave to itself is contained in the Constitution. It lays down the normative principles which are the overriding elements in the entire strategy for social change. Its emphasis on parliamentary democracy, justice, freedom and equality comprise the fundamental values to which all other processes of social change, the economic, social and cultural should be subordinated.

Democracy, equality and freedom are revolutionary ideas. These are indeed difficult to realize through a single leap forward. To realise these ideals human resources need to be generated which take time being essentially evolutionary in nature. It shows how revolution and evolution as social precesses have an intercontingent relationship. One cannot be realised in totality without the other. When we talk of revolution, we do so either in a limited sense or imply a partial aspect of revolutionary transformation. The Indian path to social transformation seeks to achieve these objectives through a series of institutional changes initiated through democratic participation. The Constitution enunciates them as establishment of a socialist democratic republic, which guarantees freedom of expression, occupation, religion and social justice to all citizens irrespective of their birth, sex and religion. It provides for measures for protective discrimination in favour of the deprived castes, classes, tribes and minorities. These objectives call for establishment of new institutions, abolition of outmoded ones and modernization of economy, technology, education and cultural life.

The industrial policy resolution of the 1950's defined that social purpose must be the guiding principle of industrial production and ownership in society. That is why a mixed economy comprising both the private sector and the public sector has been envisaged; it is also envisaged that the latter must always have a commanding position and set norms for the former. The agrarian policy envisaged abolition of all feudal institutions in ownership and production relations in agriculture. It aimed at evolving a modernised peasant proprietary agrarian structure. Both in the industrial and agrarian sector of the economy, an equitable and socially viable labour policy forms an integral element. It lays down standards of wages, conditions of service and union rights. A set of institutional measures ensure civic participation right from the village to the block, district, state and the national level in electoral decision making which are revolutionary in content and radical in practice. A variety of institutions have been provided to reinforce this process.

The social transformation envisaged through the Indian Constitution is thus pluralistic and voluntaristic with state having the crucial role of setting norms and evolving the policies. This is evident in the distribution of powers between the federal government and the states, the pattern of decentralisation of authority and the nature of the political institutions. This model also inheres a mix of the capitalistic and socialistic policies and institutions to bring about social change and modernization. In operational terms, it does not envisage violent class struggle for the achievement of objectives. On the contrary emphasis is on persuing goals through legal constitutional means and through civic protests and political mobilisation. The freedom of association and expression ensure these rights. All this implies that voluntary associations, people's movements, and political parties have to playa crucial role in ensuring that the objectives of social change as envisaged in the Constitution are realised.

The dynamic movements by the government and the state. on the one hand and by the people and their organised bodies (either as voluntary associations or as political parties or interest-group movements) on the other, form the strategy and the dialectics of this social transformation. The more effective it is, the more it ensures that those in authority or power are responsive to the needs of the people, especially the weaker sections of society. To make this model successful it assumes that the dominant classes and powerful sections of society reconcile themselves to accepting· the rational and reasonable demands made by the not so well-off sections of society for the improvement in their social, economic and cultural conditions. In other words, the democratic process of social transformation has to be *consensual* and *reconciliatory* in nature. This alone ensures social mobility, diffusion of economic and cultural privileges and resources in society contributing ultimately to the emergence of a socialist, democratic and just society. If the 'reconciliatory' process is blocked either due to political short-sightedness or sheer force of class authoritarianism, this model of social transformation breaks down resulting into authoritarian decadence or violent civil strife.

Institutional Transformation

Processes revolutionary in potential were set into motion in India soon after Independence. These comprised a series of institutional innovations. At the national scene, the electoral rights based on adult suffrage was introduced. It meant a great qualitative change in the social psychology of people and their social, cultural and political self-awareness. Social scientists have rightly called the elections in India as a measure of 'silent revolution'. It activated new social solidarities, structuration of people's aspirations. It also gave a new shape to people's social and political consciousness. It forms the single most powerful measure of regulating consensus and reconciliation in the system through operation of political processes and political mobilisation. It also subordinates the administrative and professional authority to the authority of people's representatives making the system more responsive to needs.

Institutions based on electoral participation were introduced all along the social system. In villages, the traditional panchayats based on caste, landlordism and administrative nominations were abolished. These were replaced by village panchayats based on elections open to all adult citizens in the village. This was further reinforced by establishment of councils or panchayats at levels of the block and the district. These institutions assumed great significance as they were reinforced by land reforms. The land reforms included abolition of zamindari, intermediary rights in land, tenurial reforms and ceiling on land holdings. Development Council was provided at block level comprising elected village presidents. They elected the Head of the block to look after the implementation of development policies. The power of administration was further decentralised and democratised at the district level too. Not the district collector, an administrator introduced during the colonial time, but the elected 'zila pramukh' or chief was now put in position to guide the development activities. Community Development Schemes were not only introduced for the village social and economic reconstruction. In cities and towns, they were expected to supplement the development activities of other urban agencies.

At the national level major institutional innovations included establishment of the Planning Commission and Development Council, the creation of a chain of scientific and educational institutions such as the Council for Scientific and Industrial Research; University Grants Commission, Councils for growth of research in social, historical and philosophical sciences, the Indian Councils of Medical Research etc. These institutions were to serve as agents of modernization and development in India to create a democratic, socialist republic. Special institutions and offices were created for the development of the scheduled castes, scheduled tribes, weaker sections, women, children, minorities and the backward classes. A chain of agricultural universities, scientific laboratories, institutes of technology, management and business administration were established to generate skill and human resources to accelerate industrial and agricultural growth in the country. New institutions were established to promote cultural and artistic heritage of India to safeguard against one-sided modernization. Massive economic investment was made to modernize both industry and agriculture.

Re-structuration and Contemporary Changes

Four decades after Independence these institutional changes brought about major social transformation in the Indian society. The life expectancy has risen from 32 to 56 years. The number of people who have crossed the poverty line is more than sixty percent. The domestic consumption of electricity has risen by twenty times. India has solved the problem of food shortages and ranks tenth in the world as an industrialised country. These changes have set into motion a process of social re-structuration which creates larger domains of social mobility, emergence of new caste-class alliances, new forces of social mobilization on the principles of status, class and value system. It also generates new arenas of social conflict having both beneficial and harmful consequences for social, economic, and political development of the society.

Rural Social Transformation

Institutional innovations and measures for social and economic reforms set into motion basic and irreversible changes in the rural society in India which comprises the largest social segment. During 1950's and 1960's the impact of these changes was more in the realms of values and consciousness than in the social structure. Its impact was more on people's aspirations and outlook than on their material conditions. In some parts of the country, the new electoral and political rights initiated important changes in the power structure, especially in the rural panchayats and district and state level Councils. In South India, the Brahmins and other upper caste landlords lost their power base in villages, and soon thereafter in the state political power structure. In north India, however, a ding-dong competition for power between the middle castes-classes who were formerly the tenant-eultivators of landlords and the upper caste landlords ensued in which due to better manipulative ability and demographic factors the upper caste landlords barely maintained their power and influence. The Community Development Programmes also favoured the upper caste-class groups since they had the resources to absorb technology, government aids, and they were also better educated and had good connections with the administration. The landless workers coming largely from the lower castes, were least benefited. They neither had the resources to participate in development programmes nor were they organised to bargain for a share in the new opportunities. There were as yet fewer new employment opportunities. They, therefore, maintained their bonded relationship with the upper and middle caste-classes to survive in a state of future anticipation.

The measures of decentralisation of power, land reforms and continual electoral participation, however, set into motion a process of social, economic and cultural restructuration. The patterns of feudal relationship came increasingly under pressure of challenges from different quarters. The electoral participation gave impetus to caste groups, especially those in the middle and lower ranks to form larger caste associations. The associations altered the traditional ritual-based kin-oriented nature of caste. It led to fusion and fission amongst caste groups in persuit of modern goals, such as political power, economic mobility and cultural and educational privileges. Even though anchored in traditional caste structures, these associations had a modern outlook, organisation and programme of activities. This movement started during the 1950's and 1960's and was stronger in south and western India though championed by some political parties in the north. Among the lower castes, political consciousness led to neo-Buddhist movement in western and northern India. This movement, though religious in idiom was entirely social and economic in its goals. These changes in the social structure coincided with changes in agricultural technology, educational opportunities and processes of urbanisation.

By early 1970's, the process of restructuration in both rural and urban India began to take a more concrete social shape. The investment in agriculture, development institutions and technology in villages had brought about a 'green revolution' in several parts of the country. This created sharp social cleavages and led to new class formations. An important result was the rise of the 'middle caste-class' peasantry into power often supplementing the traditional upper-caste-class landlords. Not the twice-born castes such as the Brahmins, Rajputs, Bhumihars and others but the middle-caste peasantry such as the Jats, Yadavas, Kurmis, Koeris etc. in the north, Kunbis, Patels and Marathas in the West, and Kammas, Reddis and Okkaligas in the south were in the leadership of green revolution. This development had several sociological consequences, some positive some negative in nature. On the positive side, green revolution contributed to food self-sufficiency adding economic stability to the system. It led to multiple cropping, improvement in technology, new building and construction activities, increasing employment for the working classes. It widened the scope and level of participation in development administration in villages. It led to the establishment of banking and marketing institutions, proliferation of schools and welfare activities. More importantly, green revolution reinforced a value system that was oriented to entrepreneurial initiative, emphasis on savings and austere living and stronger family and kinship bonds. The green revolution was largely carried out through a family mode of production.

These developments though beneficial to the system in the most crucial sense also generated several negative consequences. The relationship between these peasants and the landless workers became more pugnacious and exploitative with the rise in their economic and political influence and power. This is reflected in increased incidence of conflict between the landless workers and farmers in different parts of the country. It led to increased caste-class tensions in villages generating potential for violence. Increase in the income level of peasantry contributed to imitation of evils of the former landlords such as demands for dowry in marriages, conspicuous waste in ceremonies, traditional customs and beliefs. Ironically, despite economic and techonological modernization in agriculture and industries in villages a comparable degree of cultural modernization did not take place. On the contrary, conservative ideology such as casteism, communalism, masculinism and obscurantism have increased. This is so despite the fact that the youth now play an influential role in the peasant household, especially those who have some education and can successfully negotiate with institutions such as banks, marketing societies, police and revenue administration etc.

If the middle caste-class peasantry has shown upward

social mobility and greater political influence due to betterment in economic status, the position of the upper caste-class landlords in villages presents ail uneven picture of social change. This group is going through both upward and downward social mobility. They have suffered a significant degree of prolitarianization, especially in the northern states, such as Uttar Pradesh, Rajasthan and Bihar. Mostly, these comprise families which did not adjust with changed times, did not alter their style of living and work or did not move ahead through higher education and employment in non-agricultural occupations. Among such families not only the agricultural productivity is low but the increase in the size of their family over a period of time has led to fragmentation of their landholdings reducing them to the status of marginal cultivators. Often this causes a conflict between their psychological, social and cultural self-image and their objective economic condition leading to their lumpanization or even criminalization. Sometimes, this process is also repeated among other caste-class groups. Much social unrest in many northern states of India results from conflicts generated by a large section of the alienated youth from such classes. The alienation of a segment of such caste-class groups coincides with upward social mobility of its other segments which have successfully adapted to changes and reforms. The agrarian structure as demonstrated by changing size the operational holdings reveals that marginal, small as well as large size holdings have declined between 1970-71 and 1980-81, whereas the number of the medium size holding has increased during the same period, It supports the sociological observation on alienation of land both from the marginal and large landowners in favour of the medium size landowners who presumably represent the middle caste-class agrarian strata in the rural society.

This re-structuration of the upper and middle caste-class strata in villages also coincides with major social changes in its working class population which mostly comprises the scheduled castes. or other deprived lower castes. The policy of protective discrimination in their favour in operation during the past four decades has brought about a substantial change in their self-image, class consciousness and their social and economic conditions. In some regions, such as the Western Uttar Pradesh, Punjab, Haryana, Maharashtra and most of the peninsular India there has been a noticeable upward social mobility among this group with improvement in their social and economic condition. Their educational level has also gone up. Interestingly, these are also the regions where the green revolution first started. As the lower castes constitute a substantial number in these regions they tend to be better organised, have some political influence, can keep a more successful watch on the implementation of the welfare policies of the government for their benefit and can bargain better with the dominant rich and middle class peasantry. In other regions, especially the eastern Uttar Pradesh and Bihar, the condition of these classes has not yet improved. They are subject of exploitation, repression and violence. Occasionally there is eruption of violent protest, as also active mobilisation of political groups which support violence. The state of Bihar is a case of this kind in India. Here, the process of green revolution as also restructuration in social system has not yet taken place since the agrarian reform policies were subverted by feudal landlords and politicians.

The process of social restructuration is product of social and economic development. It has, however, generated social conflict in society. On the one hand, the middle caste-class peasantry clam ours for more privileges and power as revealed by the 'backward class movement' in northern India, on the other, the working classes and the scheduled castes lead organised protests and demand betterment of their social and economic conditions. The upper caste-class groups, which traditionally held power have except in some regions, a marginal role in these processes, as their success depends largely on coalition and cooptation in search of power. This is particularly true for northern India where upper caste-classes do not have a substantial rural population.

Urbanization, Industrialization and Social Re-structuration

Modernization in India is symbolised by green revolution in villages. It is also organically linked with the process of urbanization and industrialisation. During the past four decade there has been massive growth in urban centres and industrial units. The urban population which in 1901 stood at 25.9 millions, in 1951 at 62.4 millions rose to 156.2 millions in 1981. It comprised 17.3 percent of the total population in 1951; in 1981 it had risen to 23.3 percent of the total population. More importantly, the composition of older cities has radically changed with pressure of migrant population. Between 1951-1981, about 355 new towns emerged in India and the percentage of class-I towns roughly trebled. Similarly. substantial industrial expansion has taken place. The figures of joint-stock companies both public and private show that their number in 1971 was to the tune of 30,461, and it rose to 118,305 in 1985 (December). The growth in private companies has been more rapid in terms of numbers than in the public companies. The number of labourers working in organised sector roughly doubled during 1961 and 1984 rising from 12.09 millions to 24.2 millions.

Sociologically, these changes have had major implications for social restructuration not only in these sectors of activity but also in the society in general. Expansion in industrial activities enlarged the social base of industrial workers. More important than this, it created a large number of industrial-urban middle class in India The rank of traditional industrial capitalist classes was joined by a new breed of inercantile capitalists and industrial entrepreneurs. Their number runs in thousands. The impetus given by government's industrial policy led to the rise of a new class of capitalist entrepreneurs in the corporate sector. This trend coincided with swelling of the ranks of professional classes in the domains of technology, education, science, law, medicine, civil services, army and police services, journalism and architecture etc.. The urban middle class comprises these upward mobile groups which represent the process of modernization in India today.

The rise of these classes is a result of investment in development and modernization since Independence. It is indicative of social mobility and restructuration going on in society. It contributes to and represents the outcome of the processes of social change. Let us understand the social base of this new professional and industrial middle class. It comes largely from the upper caste-class strata of the traditional Indian society. Its outlook and ideology is highly utilitarian which makes it ready to absorb modern technology and use all opportunities for upward social mobility. Its social outlook and-belief systems are, however, traditional, rooted in religiosity and tend to be conservative. Its growth does not represent only change but also continuity, a continuity which symbolises social resilience but is often anchored in disvalues. Opportunism, obscurantism and corrupt practices have penetrated a segment of this class because of the nebulous nature of the ideological anchorage it has in the value system of a modern society. The new urban middle class, therefore, is a measure of both India's development as well, as its underdevelopment. The underdevelopment can be witnessed in the fast expansion of slum population in most cities, specially in the Indian metropolises. It can be seen in the rise in the number of alienated youth, and social crimes.

Cultural Changes and Social Restructuration

The contradictions of social development are also reflected in the cultural changes that are taking place in India today. Both in the rural and urban social systems the quest for economic and social modernization has activated cultural forces which legitimise values like acquisitiveness, opportunistic utilitarianism, revivalism, communalism and primordialism. These have resulted from social restructuration in society during the past forty years. The rural development symbolised by green revolution, and urban development reflected in entrepreneurialism and professionalism have ironically generated a sense of narrow utilitarianism instead of liberal and cosmopolitan values of modernization, This has probably resulted due to the lack of clear ideological orientation in the processes of economic and social development. It may also be attributed to the inevitable pangs of capitalist development in a society professing the goals of a socialist democratic transformation.

The cultural changes in India today mirror both forces of resilience and transformation. The resilience can be seen in the expanding role of religion and its expressions in people's life. Religion gets equal patronage from political leaders, corporate executives, professionals and capitalists. Education of science and technology does not seem to displace religion from people's private and public life. Instead, a unique mode of dualistic coexistence of scientific rationality in instrumental roles with religious values in fundamental domains of life has been worked out by most professionals in India who occupy scientific and technological offices. The same is true in social life; such as family, caste and kinship organisations. The traditional cultural values of instrumental nature such as those related to health, food, nutrition, transport and communication are, however, being fast replaced by new. rational instrumental values of science and technology. One finds this reflected in high degree of acceptance by people of modern medical science, new varieties of food and food technology, material culture, and their acceptance of new modes of information and communication. The commitment to modern values is also reflected in electoral politics, new management structures and scientific and technological institutions of society. It is indicative of the resilience of the traditional values and institutions which accommodate and adopt new values of social and cultural modernization. The basic pluralism of Indian social structure and its inter-structural autonomy facilitated the initial process of cultural modernization when India was exposed to the West through colonization. After Independence, cultural modernization became more participatory and less exclusive with mass participation in institutions of social, economic and cultural development. This has enlarged the base of people's participation in modern ways of life and sharpened their political consciousness and sense of identity. It has also set into motion new values as well as disvalues as the process of social restructuration takes place in society on a meaningful scale. Revivalism, casteism, communalism and regionalism are some of the disvalues which have emerged as a result of this development.

Communalism is a particularly powerful social disvalue which has continually been active in the Indian process of social and cultural modernization. Its historical roots go far back to British colonialism which gave birth to this ideology in order to divide and rule over the Indian people. Their geopolitical interests later led them to strengthen communalism in India and divide the country on religious lines before departing from the subcontinent. Indian leadership never accepted the ideology of two-nation theory based on religion and its surrogate ideology of communalism. It was historically refuted when Bangladesh came into existence. Communalism, however, once implanted in the mind of the people has continued to torment and thwart the process of cultural modernization in the society. It has during the past four decades taken a complex social and ideological form. In the first instance, it gets mixed up ideologically with the process of social restructuration in society. In this form, it serves as a disguise for class and interest group ideology. The new middle classes of various religious communities exploit the communal identities of the poorer sections of their co-religionists. The deprivations of these communities in social and economic fields are attributed to religious minority status in contravention-of the objective situations. In this sense communalism does often function as false consciousness. In other situations, communalism is simply engineered by opportunistic political and economic interests of contending groups and factions within a political party or by political parties. Communalism emerges in India as most important threat to cultural modernization. It is a complex process but its causes generally subsist in the contradictions generated by the forces of social restructuration. The uneven pace of social mobility and a sense of deprivation by groups and communities which perceive the chances of their status mobility blocked is probably an important contingent factor which fuels communal prejudices and makes it possible for opportunistic elements in society to exploit it. This coincides with new assertiveness of socially mobile sections from. among the minority communities which contend for higher social and economic position and treat communalism as a tool for social mobilisation. This breeds communal strife, sometimes communal violence.

Another form of communalism which is of recent origin is that of religious fundamentalism. It has both national and international dimensions. It comprises propagation of a worldview of religion to which according to its belief all other aspects of life must be subordinated, be they political, economic, social or cultural. It is in complete contradiction to the scientific rational worldview of secularism, a cultural policy, to which India is committed. In India, since the past few decades there has been a rise in fundamentalist movements, but these too have links with political and economic issues. Whether it is Sikh fundamentalism in Punjab or Muslim fundamentalism in parts of the country, these movements have arisen only after the communities concerned have gone through a certain level of social mobility, economic development and rise in aspirations. This process, therefore, indirectly confirms the view that like other forms of communalism religious fundamentalism too has its roots in the social and economic restructuration of the contemporary Indian society. The measures to overcome this too will have to be linked with policies of economic and social development in furtherance of a secular cultural policy.

Patterns of Contemporary Social Change

The pattern of social change that one witnesses in India today reflects elements of continuity with modernization. The continuities can be discerned in areas of social structure and belief systems which show resilience. It can be seen in the adaptive mode of modernization through the medium of traditional institutions. The role of joint family system in maintaining and promoting entrepreneurial activities both in industry and agriculture, the uses of religious and ritualistic symbols in modern modes of communication of highly political and educational messages, the use of caste and kinship in the mobilisation of people for political, developmental and other forms of associative and professional persuits, etc. are its examples. There is no linear change in India from tradition to modernity, instead we find a process of modernization of tradition.

After seventies, however, we witness social movements in India which out-cross caste and kinship ties. More associations and professional bodies of scientists and experts; have emerged which do not mirror in their organisation and activities elements of caste, kinship or regional identities as the caste association did in the 1960's. Social movements of professionals, youths and women which cut across caste, region and religion have emerged. Several popular people's movements in various parts of the country have sprung up which have as their objective popularization of modern scientific outlook, concern for social ecology, social justice and equality. This has activated in India a process of social change where not *community* but *category* becomes an important nodal point of social mobilization, interest articulation and organisation. The significance of communatarian social structures such as family, caste, tribe and kingroup is still predominant, but increasingly new social arenas are being mobilised for economic, organisational, professional and technological achievements whose membership is not by primordial identity but on the basis of class, professional skill, economic interests, gender and age or other civic principles. This has resulted as the pace of economic, technological and scientific development has become stronger in the country.

It is in this context that the role of class formation can be examined in the analysis of social change in the contemporary India. There is massive data and theoretical material on class structure and the process of social change in India. The rural, corporate and professional sectors of Indian society have been studied using the class model for the analysis of social change. Obviously, the significance of class as a structural concept for understanding the continuity and change in society increases more when it is viewed as a *process*, a *reality in a state of flux and formation* rather than as a finished product. The notions of modes of production offer advantages for the analysis of processes of social change to the extent that the conceptual packages and operational tools employed in this model view social reality in a state of *becoming* rather than *being*, a feature from which only a few studies using this model do not suffer. The

Indian social transformation is not such that can be adequately explained by a linear model of transition from one mode of production such as 'feudalistic' to another such as the 'capitalist'. It is more complex, and at each stage of social existence one may witness more than a single mode of production. A 'feudal' mode of production might inhere 'capitalist' elements. The 'ancient' mode of production such as bondage and collectivism on the principle of kinship or *biradari* might coexist with capitalist mode of rational allocation of technological resources for production. For similar reasons, some social scientists have even ventured to speak of a *jati* or caste mode of production. Conceptually, therefore, in the analysis of contemporary processes of social change in India what is important is to fully grasp the *process* of continuity and change in society. The more social scientists are faithful to this task the better models of understanding social transformation they may be able to evolve. Analysis of social change through mode of production can be treated only as the first step towards greater challenges that might be encountered in its operationalisation.

The Indian persuit for social development and social change is orientated to socialist transformation within the framework of a parliamentary democracy. This itself puts limits on the policies and strategies for social change. These policies consciously inhere elements which are both capitalistic and socialistic in persuits. In many sectors of social life and economy such as agriculture, the policy of peasant proprietorship on capitalist lines was followed by land reforms such as ceiling on land holdings in persuit of socialist goals. This has strengthened middle class capitalism as also created dominant caste and kingroups akin to feudalistic social formations. The concepts of feudalism and capitalism are, therefore, in the Indian context of social change more sensitising than definitive or explanatory in character.

Chapter 3

Social Transformation of the Indian Society

Momentous changes have taken place in India since independence. These changes offer today numerous challenges and new opportunities. Their objective analysis is necessary to evaluate and to set out new policy directions to augment the processes of social transformation. To accomplish this task a sound 'theoretical perspective' is essential. In its absence one could be misled to the mistaken attitudes of either pessimism or optimism or cynicism about the future of social transformation in India. This has indeed been happening as the literature on social change indicates. It may, however, be noted that social sciences are at their weakest in formulating a 'theory' of social change as such. In contradistinction, they have achieved substantial credibility in postulating a theory of social structure, forms of kinship, family, linguistic structures and modes of economy. In the analysis of change, however, social scientists encounter formidable challenges.

Most theories of social change serve as constructs that *sensitise* but do not *explain*. This is equally true for macro-theories of social change as also those with smaller range. In such a situation, analysis of social change suffers from various types of fallacies, which the social scientists and public would have to guard against in order to have an objective view of social transformation. Some of the more common fallacies in the analysis of change are those of dilettantism, ideological mystification and the structuralist mode of thinking. There are indeed areas where the dilettante has an advantage over the specialist. But dilettantism is the creed of the anti-intellectual who flourishes under specific socio-historical conditions of society. Dilettantism is bred by a political culture of non-organic or partisan mould, where ideologies noursihed by petty prejeudices prevail over objective, consensual and apperceptive mode of thinking.

As Max Weber rightly said: "Almost all sciences owe something to dilettantes, often very valuable viewpoints. But dilettantism as a leading principle would he the end of science." Some specific expressions of the fallacy of dilettantism in India are the communal, sectarian and primordial biases in the interpretations of social change. Not facts but prejudices, not reason but antipathy, not history but biography are the guides for dilettante's 'generalisations' on social change and its directions.

Yet another fallacy in the explanation of social change is that of ideological mystification. Indeed, dilettante also mystifies but he has no ideology. The ideological mystification has its origin in the professions and the traditions of learning in social sciences. Its biases have their roots in epistemic, methodological and operational foundations of social sciences which are socially and politically conditioned. Myriad examples of such theorising on the issues of development and social change can be found in the literature of social sciences. Ideologies are normative constructs and introduce culturological fallacies in the interpretation of social processes.

Another fallacy in the analysis of social change is that of the 'structuralist mode of thinking'. This belongs to the sociological tradition of not looking at social reality as 'processes' or in their states of 'becoming', but as structures of abstract sets of relationships. Under its conceptual premise social change is studied by formulating sets of structural typologies rather than analysis of the social processes going on in society. Emphasis is on abstract structures rather than on social formations. It leads to several erroneous views on the study of social change. First is a questioning attitude towards the study of social change as a worthwhile task for sociologists as such, a position taken by a few sociologists having structuralist theoretical orientation. Their interest is in the discovery of the 'principles' of social order rather than 'processes' of social change, which they think are rooted in ideologies. To them, comparison is tantamount to the study of change. Secondly, the structuralist analysis of change attempts to comprehend change by postulating types of 'system-states', such as 'tradition' and 'modernity' or 'feudalism' and 'capitalism', etc. The extent to which these system-states are postulated as rational 'types' or as ideological constructs without the sense of historicity they serve to obfuscate rather than reveal the processes of social change.

These fallacies about the understanding of social change perform different functions in the Indian society. Dilettantism is the product of an ideology of change that is indifferent to the goals of social justice and equality as postulated in the Constitution. Its champions are the new rich and the new middle classes. The fallacy of ideological mystification results from the partisan character of social sciences and social conditioning of the theory of change. This may range from the ideological differentiation of social scientists to their differentiation based on their social origin. At the international level, the biases in the explanation of social change may also result from either misplaced transplantations of alien models of study or through it in the projection of an ideology. The fallacy of the 'structuralist mode of thinking' however, has as its limitation a mode of explanation of social change which is devoid of historicity and neglects the concrete social processes leading to academic formalism and consequently, empty generalisations.

The Initial Conditions of Social Change

To understand the sociological dimensions of change in India it is necessary to grasp the concrete process of restructuration going on in society. These processes have been set into motion under specific historical contexts of public policy and national ideology. Historical forces define the initial social conditions from which the processes of social transformation and restructuration began in India. One has to draw both from history and sociology in order to understand the shape of these initial conditions. Its main, feature has been the principles of inter-structural autonomy in the social system. The main structures concerned are the social stratification, political system and the cultural ideology. Caste comprises the central principle of social stratification, and traditionally it enjoyed great deal of internal autonomy. Being regional in character the caste panchayats functioned as relatively autonomous economic, cultural and judicial systems well upto the 1930's. Only in exceptional circumstances did the members of a caste go in for appeal to the institutions of the state (king) for redressal of grievances. The relationship between the state and the representatives of the cultural tradition—the priests, was also governed by relative autonomy. The Indian polity was never a theodicy; it always accommodated plural cultural and religious traditions. The process of social change ushered in by the British rule set into motion social and cultural dynamics that started reorganisation of this pattern.

The inter-structural autonomy of the social components in the traditional Indian society has deeply influenced the nature and direction of social change. Their role could be evaluated through various stages of historical transformation. The first stage coincided with the beginning of the Western contact through British rule which set the pace for cultural renaissance, initial industrialisation and growth of new political consciousness culminating in national freedom movement. These forces brought about major changes in the Indian society, specially in the areas of institution-building for a civic society such as the growth of modern education and judicial-administrative structures. It was marked paradoxically by a process of de-industrialisation and ruralisation of economy on the one hand and the emergence of a colonial mode of industrialisation and modernization on the other. These innovations convulsed the traditional social structure, led to downward mobility of several privileged classes and families and selective upward mobility of others drawn from the traditional business classes, literati and feudal nobility. This mobility created new classes of educationists, administrators, professionals, businessmen, company agents and others who took advantage of the opportunities available in the early phases of colonial transformation.

The emergence of these social groups together with cultural awakening and reform movements in various parts of the country prepared the ground for political awareness and national movement. This became a potent source of social and ideological mobilisation intensifying the sense of collective self-awareness. The movement led by Gandhiji imparted this process an ideological shape. A strategy not only for political independence but social, economic and cultural modernisation of society was evolved. The emphasis on the involvement of women, members of the weaker sections, peasants and workers reflected this ideological perspective. Political leadership at the local, regional and national level emerged. Leadership also emerged from among the weaker sections, women and tribal groups. A substantial section of middle classes comprising educationists, professionals, bureaucrats and businessmen had already set forth a new process of social mobility. This process of change, however, had a segmentary character. It did not affect the large parts of rural peasantry, working classes, the scheduled castes and tribes. The national movement too in many ways had a segmentary character, despite periods of mass mobilization. This is being highlighted by recent studies in subaltern history. Possibly, the inter-structural autonomy of the Indian social system was responsible for this. It made it possible that selective modernization could take place. Along the enclaves of rapid social transformation it left massive areas of society untouched by winds of change.

This elitist or segmentary nature of social change had its positive features. It helped galvanise social energies of the people to fight against foreign rule without maximising internal schisms. The British policy of divide and rule only partially succeeded. The evolution of a constitutional and democratic strategy of social transformation has been possible also due to this social feature. It kept the pace of transformation within the tolerance limit of the culture and society. The process of change could start and filter down without major breakdown in the social structure, and without the loss of cultural identity.

Independence and the Strategy of Social Transformation

The strategy of social change after Independence underwent fundamental changes. The state took upon itself the responsibility of conscious planning of social transformation. Its objectives were the creation of a society based on democratic political participation, social justice and cultural and religious pluralism within the framework of a secular state. Steps were taken to abolish institutions which traditionally perpetuated exploitation and inequality. A policy framework was introduced to strengthen institutions which served the objectives of justice in society. It meant also the abolition of the age-old principles of inter-structural autonomy in the Indian society. The principles of inequality based on caste, birth, religion and sex were in normative sense, derecognised if not successfully abolished. The new institutions which sought to-replace them implied changes in society which had very revolutionary implications.

The Constitution of India broadly lays down these objectives. In some areas the policy of change began to show immediate results. These were electoral politics, agrarian reforms, industrial and economic expansion and investment ill education, science and technology. All these coincided with an expanding role of communication and media participation. The electoral politics, apart from its liberating psychological effects on the minds of people released new social energy in society. This was compounded by abolition of the intermediary rights in land, introduction of panchayat raj and community development schemes in villages. The rural areas were thus exposed to major forces of social change.

However, the nature of social change in India's villages during the 1950's and 1960's indicates uneven impact on its social structure. The domination of the traditional castes and classes continued despite social and economic reforms. The electoral challenges from the lower castes, the ex-tenantry, working classes and the weaker sections did not alter the traditional power structure. The benefits of extension work in agriculture, animal husbandry, irrigation, marketing, credit and cooperatives were monopolised by the traditional upper caste rich strata. More significant changes in the power structure of the rural society took place in the southern states than in the northern ones, because of the differences in the caste demography. In this region too, spectacular patterns of changes emerged later as the investment made during the 1950's and 1960's matured in the 1970's and 1980's. Social mobility during the first two decades after independence was slow and mainly confined to the upper castes and classes. The poorer sections of peasantry, agricultural workers and Harijans did feel the liberating impact of the new reforms psychologically, and in some measure culturally, but its overall impact on their status, power and. income remained marginal.

Similar processes had been taking place in urban centres. The urban change during this period has been termed as 'over urbanisation'. It meant city-ward migration of population without its occupational integration in urban industrial work force. It led to urban degradation, exploitation and impoverishment. The increase in entrepreneurship and industrial investment was confined to the upper classes. The opportunities of education, especially in science, technology, medicine and professions continued to be the preserve of the privileged groups. Some openings were, however, found by the agricultural labourers, peasants, scheduled castes and tribes to send their children to the primary and secondary schools and a very small proportion of them went to colleges or institutions of higher education. Few among them could survive upto university level of education. Sociologically, however, even the school and college drop-outs served important function later as catalysers of social, economic and cultural change in their society.

Thus, the changes during the first two decades after independence were also segmentary as in the past. There were, however, some major differences: the scope and potential of the social transformation now was much larger and the aspiration for social mobility had ceased to be segmentary. It had assumed a truly structural dimension engulfing the whole of the society. This, with rising population, preponderance of the young in society, greater political participation, exposure to media, such as radio, newspapers, magazines and public meetings led to a new social and political awareness. The welfare policies of reservations for the scheduled castes and tribes, land reforms and developmental planning led to the emergence of a category of people from among the lower strata who were self-conscious of their deprivation, could assume leadership role of their community and mobilise them for organisation and protest. The release of these social forces also coincided with major investment in science and technology, in agriculture, industry and health. The cumulative result of these have shown results during the 1970's and 1980's. In many rural regions there has been a 'green revolution' and the rise of new peasant middle classes. In urban-industrial domain a new mercantile entrepreneurial class has emerged. However, in the realm of culture and the national ideology, the values of secularism, social justice, consensus and participation have increasingly come under strain. These spell out serious consequences for the political culture and its future in India. We have to understand these forces, redefine our strategies and plan for the future.

Rural Social Transformation

Today, the changes in rural India, which constitutes the dominant sector of our society, are bringing about a process of rapid social restructuration. It is leading to a breakdown in the segmentary mode of social change, rise of new middle classes to power, massive absorption of science and technology in agriculture and substantial changes in values and beliefs. The green revolution signifies not merely growth in agricultural production but also the use of new technology and social relationships in production processes. These developments make the new phase of changes in rural economy and society a distinct process. A new interaction among technology, social relationship and culture is now taking place in the rural society. This has resulted into social mobility, emergence .of new power structure and mode of exploitation of the deprived classes. It has generated new contradictions in the rural society.

Socially, the green revolution has been basically a contribution of the middle caste peasantry, who have had traditionally a strong attachment to land and agriculture as a mode of life and livelihood. The Jats, Kurmis, Yadavas in the north, the Kunbis, Patels and Patidars in Gujarat, the Marathas in Maharashtra, the Kammas, Reddis and Rajus in Andhra Pradesh, the Vanniyars and Nadars in Tamilnadu, etc. have been the leaders of green revolution. It is anchored in the traditional peasant caste structure. Yet, the green revolution marks a basic departure from the traditional pattern. The family mode of production continues, but authority has passed from the older to the younger generation. The new agriculture requires the skill in the peasant to negotiate with banks, revenue authorities, police administration, marketing bodies and block development administration. The new peasant is required to consult the experts and technicians for irrigation, soil testing, the use of fertilisers and seeds. This could not be handled with facility by the older generation of peasants. This role is increasingly being performed by the younger generation which is college or school educated or even a drop-out from these institutions. This change is also reflected in the Panchayat elections and the rural electoral politics in general.

The green revolution has led to the consolidation of the status of the middle peasantry as a dominant class. But the rural poor too have got more organised. They too have now a youthful leadership which deals with agencies of development, political parties and institutions of law and order. The upper caste-class groups which traditionally dominated have now been either replaced by the middle peasantry or have to compete with them to maintain their traditional status and power. They employ a variety of strategies of cooptation, compromises and occasional confrontations. These. triangular sets of social forces in rural society, which are particularly prominent in the northern states lead increasingly to social polarisation, large scale migration to cities, social tensions and erosion of political culture. The quality of the relationship between the middle caste peasantry and the lower castes has particularly declined and is marked by exploitation and violence.

The peasantry have had a tradition of Bhakti movements or other reform movements in various parts of the country; their subculture has always had a strong ethic of workmanship, industry, frugality and conservative utilitarianism. These values combined with the social processes of upward mobility and social, political and economic dominance have given birth to a cultural milieu which is more self-centred and antipathic to values of accommodation and social justice. Their relationship with the agricultural working classes, the lower castes and Harijans is increasingly that of aggressiveness and antipathy. This is being reciprocated by the lower castes and working classes as well, leading to a sharp decline in the cultural ethos of the rural society. A situation is emerging in which the dominant classes do not take kindly to policies of protective discrimination and the weaker sections do not accept the legitimacy of such reform measures. The result is more conflict and less consensus on social issues. This happens when more and more mobility and development is taking place.

We see in this process mixed blessings for society in general. It indicates a remarkable process of restructuration and social mobility. It reflects the rise of an economic ethic which is productive and generates surpluses and capital accumulation. It has already achieved a degree of shift of authority ill favour of the younger people; it reinforces the resiliences of the social system for selective absorption of technology, leading to high productivity and growth in agriculture. These changes have contributed to the upward mobility of the middle castes on the one hand, and on the other sharpened the self-awareness of the lower castes and poorer classes. They have resorted to large scale migration to towns, cities and other regions of India in search of employment and better opportunities. These developments, however, also coincide with negative social processes. A change in the value system and ideology of the people which promotes localism, casteism, and communalism has taken place. This results into conflictual and exploitative relationship between the peasant classes and the rural poor. It also results in negative perceptions of the work, status and role of women. Its cultural outcome is that of revival of masculinism, increase in dowry system and cultural conservatism. Thus, social changes also have brought about conflict and maladjustment in the structure of society.

Mercantile and Industrial Entrepreneurship

The massive investment in industry and technology which took place during the first two decades after independence has resulted into significant development in industrial activities and rise of entrepreneurial classes in the urban areas. The size of the urban middle classes has more than doubled. The numbers of entrepreneurs of small and medium size as also those having broader social background have grown in substantial measure. This has come with the rise in commercial and industrial activities. Compared to the traditional business classes who largely had their social origin in the trading castes or communities, the new merchant class comes from a diverse and broader social background. It has contributed to the weakening of the segmentary social base of the commercial and industrial capitalism in India, a process similar to that taking place in the rural society. The growth in the size of the services, professions and administrative or developmental bureaucracy reflects the social dynamism and mobility in the urban-industrial sector of society. Slowly the process of mercantile capitalism growing and maturing into industrial capitalism is taking place in India. Today it is happening on a much larger scale than it did during the British rule or the initial decades after independence.

This process should be analysed together with those of the demographic transition and urbanisation. As the census figures reveal, a proliferation of townships with growth in economic activities and rise in transport and market facilities has taken place. The medium size cities have grown into cities of million population or into urban metropolises. The rise in urban population, mostly of an unplanned nature, has put severe pressure on urban facilities, services, housing, sanitation, health and ecology. It has led to the proliferation of slums, over-urbanisation, increase in crime and other problems. The sheer weight of unplanned growth in urban population puts the civic values and amenities into jeopardy. Speculative and clandestine commercial activities get linked up with exploitation of the urban poor. It breeds cultural anomie, promotes sectarianism, communalism and regionalism.

These negative aspects of urbanisation and industrialisation go together with positive growth in entrepreneurship and industry. An urban middle class has also emerged with the rise of mercantile and industrial capitalism. The social base of the middle classes has thus broadened both in the urban and rural society. The cultural background and ethos of this middle class has not, however, been studied fully but it is obvious that it sets the trend for the contemporary process of modernization. What is its ideology? This question assumes significance for analysis of the existing patterns and future directions of social change in India. The cultural values of the emergent rural middle classes show sharper contradictions between their ideology and 'national' goals of social transformation. Is the cultural ethos of the urban middle classes much different in nature? This is an important question, and calls for serious investigation by social scientists.

The historical context of the urban-industrial transformation today is different. The entrepreneurs and capitalist classes that have arisen during the past three decades have a different value system. The traditional business classes had interacted closely with national movement and its political and economic ideology. The new business classes despite being a product of the national economic and social policies have a value structure that is more inwardly directed. It is often governed by short-run business interests rather than long-term national economic and social goals commensurate with national policies. The new capitalist class has grown under the protection of nation's economic policies and has enjoyed political support, but its commitment to the cosmopolitan values of national development, social justice, welfare, liberalism and rationality has yet to be established. The evidence often suggests its negative or indifferent commitment to these values. Industrial capitalism has not successfully grown in any society without a strong rational ethical tradition and discipline in personal and public conduct. The ethical base of the emerging rural and urban capitalism has a complex character. While in some areas such as motivation or commitment, discipline of work and its technical efficiency it matches standards of high quality, its functioning in the social context deviates from such norms to a significant degree. It has yet to evolve a rational-ethical worldview in harmony with the values and ideologies of the nation state. This is especially so in regard to values of distributive justice, social responsibility and non-sectarianism.

A process of social restructuration is taking place in the urban and industrial sector of our life. It symbolises social dynamism, mobility and growth and yet, it serves as a harbinger of increasing cultural disvalues and anomie. The increase in the social and ideological chasm between the urban rich and middle classes and the urban poor and the weaker sections indicates it. It is compounded by the high degree of communication exposure, mass media participation and political activism. The professional and intellectual classes who could normally perform integrative role as catalysts of modernization and positive social values have a fractured moral existence. Studies of the professions of medicine, law, science and technology, humanities and social sciences reveal a schismatic character of its ideology. It has been observed that:

> "In terms of technical expertise, skill and organisation process of professionalization does contribute to modernization. Some professions do so more than others. In the former category are the professions of management, science and technology. The medical, legal and other professions come next. In terms of ideology and social structure the nature of modernization that professions have promoted in India is highly class-oriented, is segmentary in character and contributes to a structure of social, economic and political domination which reinforces social and economic inequalities. It also creates a subculture of modernity with a high degree of dependency... Coming from a narrow class base, the professions in India, with few exceptions, are insensitive to the needs of a majority of the poor people in rural and urban areas." (Singh, Yogendra: 1986)

Cultural and Ideological Transformation

Yet, there have emerged recently new cultural and ideological movements in India. The two important cultural sources which initiate this process are those of science and religious values. The fear of social scientists that religious values in India would hamper the growth of science and technology has been disproved. Yet, traditional values do retard the process of institutionalisation of science in our social life. The view that science would displace religion from human life too has been disproved. In India, as in many other societies, modernization processes initiated by science and technology proceed along with adaptive changes in religious values and beliefs. Paradoxically in most of the contemporary world, advance in science is not able to check the rise of sectarian, racial, and other fundamentalist beliefs. The cultural transformation in our society, which has made successful adaptive synthesis between scientific-technological and traditional values, too now shows tensions of rising fundamentalism.

This paradox has its basis probably in the worldview of science itself. The pedagogy of science has its limits. It does not claim to offer nor does it have the capacity to offer, explanation of ultimate riddles of human condition rooted in the fundamental values, It offers tentative though successful solutions to issues related to the instrumental values in human life. That is why science reaches its peak of success in the realm of technology without, however, offering equally credible sets of fundamental or categorical values. The values that derive legitimacy from religion or tradition are of a fundamental nature. Science can offer neither confirmation nor disconfirmation of such values. In the social framework, therefore, technological values derived from science tend to coexist with religious practices and traditions. Science does, however, seriously challenge those religious or cultural practices which are based on erroneous instrumental values in life. Societies shed such values increasingly in the process of modernisation, but the basic core of the fundamental values of religion go unaffected, both existentially and epistemologically. Moreover, as religious values remain outside the scope of scientific proof or disproof they are subject to diverse forms of mystification.

The disvalues of religion or its narrow fundamentalist, communal and sectarian manifestations have their origin in the process of mystification. Mystification is rampant in the contemporary historical context of religion. We define. mystification as a process by which values which belong to the instrumental domains, such as economic, political, racial or communitarian, etc., are lifted from their relevant contexts and transfigurated into categorical values by an interpretive fiat or demogogy, Thus, issues which normally belong to the instrumental or rational realm, and could be sorted out as such are withdrawn from this domain and passed on to the domain of unreason. This defines the character of fundamentalist ideology. One has to investigate the social conditions under which this transfiguration takes place to strike at the root of fundamentalism and its problems in modern society. Its origin lies in exploitation of people's anxieties and frustrations on account of their human condition, existential, social and spiritual. A major part of these anxieties arises from social inequalities and exploitation, and the powerful vested interests who. feel threatened by social mobility and freedom.

The process of social restructuration going on in our society today is full of contradictions. We witness economic growth with increasing social inequalities, political freedom with fore-closure of existential opportunities, changes in values and definition of the self without elasticity in social structure, or its power base and social mobility without corresponding evolution of organic consciousness. The segmentary nature of traditional social structure with its inter-structural autonomy had the advantage of encapsulating the impact of changes at the selective levels of social structure. That is how the first stage of modernisation could proceed in India without major upheavals in society. At the present stage of modernization the very principles of inter-structural autonomy are breaking down. In fact, this is how it should be, in order to establish a democratic, free and just social order. But this process is releasing such social, cultural and emotional forces in society that render the rise in expectations so fast and intense that the process of social re-structuration cannot keep pace with this transition. It thus retards the growth of organic social and cultural consciousness. This is evident from the rise of communalism, casteism, tribalism and fundamentalism in our society.

The accelerated pace of social restructuration which has enlarged the size of the rural and urban middle classes, encouraged entrepreneurial activities and the process of urbanisation, etc., has not, however, reinforced cultural values of secularism, justice and equality. It has encouraged an ideology that is non-liberal and non-cosmopolitan, and the neo-conservative sham-meritocracy, utilitarian opportunism and ethical fuzziness are its main features. The poorer and exploited classes perceive in this cultural profile of the middle classes a rejection of their identity. Their cultural perceptions suffer a semiotic break which leads them to 'subalternity' or a search for counter models of values. Insurgent ideology is a product of such subalternity. We have observed it happening in the ideology of the caste system. There is a movement among the scheduled castes to reject the Brahmanical model of pollution-purity for a model based on class exploitation. The alienative cultural processes have obstructed the growth of cosmopolitan cultural tradition commensurate with our national ideology.

Traditionally, the organic cultural values were sustained in India by creative linkages between the folk art-forms, its rich oral tradition and the classical art-forms of the elite. There was a syncretic relationship between the two cultural traditions. The local and the cosmoplitan cultural traditions interacted together in their diversity and unity constituting a whole. Modernization process introduces the technological and structural forces that put strains both on the folk and the elite traditions of culture. The pace of social re-structuration, the emergence of new classes, and the decline of traditional cultural institutions exemplify this process. Social mobility, migration and occupational diversification break the traditional institutional bases of art and culture. Society thus faces dual cultural crisis, decline of the traditional forms and institutions on the one hand and on the other the feebleness of the new cultural institutions and forms. Here, the role of modern communication technology both of the print and electronic media becomes immense. Not only are the institutional alternatives to- be innovated to continue the process of creative cultural evolution but also our cultural identity and heritage needs to be maintained through the autonomy of the media software. This would particularly apply to the radio and television in India, particularly the latter which has a great potential as a catalyser of integrative cultural consciousness.

Challenges and Opportunities

The social transformation going on in India poses many challenges and offers new opportunities. The challenges are about the understanding or analysis of the intrinsic character of social changes, its contradictions and about evolving successful strategies to overcome them. The first is the dilettante perception of change which offers a partisan perspective and is devoid of historical sensitivity. Then there are ideological interpretations of social change based on alien models of analysis. A more common error in the study of social changes is that of the 'structuralist mode of thinking' where processes of change are analysed with the help of reified categories of social structure and values. Social indicators are used that are pure abstractions from reality bereft of the sense of history and fail to capture the complexities of social processes. It is, therefore, necessary to focus upon the concrete processes of social-transformation in their historicity for a balanced and objective perspective on social change.

Once we view social changes in terms of the concrete processes we capture its substantive reality more objectively. Most processes of change both in the' rural, urban and tribal areas have resulted from the investment in development, economic, social and cultural. This development itself has set into motion process of social restructuration, new class formation and social mobility. Technology, population growth and entrepreneurial revival have added new pace to these changes. The nature of social transformation has increasingly challenged the traditional principles of interstructural autonomy and segmentary functioning of institutions. It has put new adaptive pressures on a segmentary structures of society such as caste, ethnicity and community. New demands are made on the function and ideology of these entities as adaptive tensions of change widen the social and cultural hiatus between groups and strata. These changes have a dualistic character; first, they result from the uses of science and technology as rational tools of production and learning, and secondly, their ideological or symbolic universe deviates from the ethos of science and tends to be conservative and noncosmopolitan. This breeds tremendous contradictions in the process of social transformation. It enhances the tendency among the deprived groups to adopt 'insurgent' or 'subaltern' strategies of counter ideologies, which too are intrinsically noncosmopolitan, in some cases even fundamentalist or communal in nature.

These challenges if understood in their historico-sociological context indicate also the opportunities that our society has today to correct the imbalances arising in the process of social transformation. We have today a substantial base of skilled manpower in our society. We need to mobilise it to combat the disvalues and conflicts arising out of the process of social change. This holds true particularly in the domains of cultural ideology. To counter the emergent disvalues of communalism, fundamentalism and neo-conservatism it is necessary that we make increasing use of modern institutional and technological means. Along with the modernization of educational processes and its content, there is a need for a people's non-political movement. The involvement of the electronic and print media in this process is of utmost necessity. We have to initiate a movement as it were, comprising the youth, the rural masses and the intellectuals towards reaffirmation of our national cultural ideology. This ideology is broadly defined in our Constitution and in our heritage of national movement. Secularism, socialism, equality and democratic participation are ideals which cannot be maintained without our commitment to this cultural ideology.

Another area where we have new opportunities for our goals of social transformation is that of human resource mobilization. Ours is a society dominated by the youthful population. It represents tremendous human energy which has not yet been cannalised for social purposes. In the absence of a national policy in this regard it finds random expressions in some positive and many negative directions. It is often misused by communal, fundamentalist and sectarian forces. To galvanise this energy it is essential that apart from the platform of political parties, purposeful voluntary organisations should be brought into this field of activity. The stable modernization of a society rests not so much on the shoulders of state or its governmental agencies as on those of the active and watchful chain of voluntary organisations of people which are organised around objectives as diverse as are the goals of modernization in society. We have been singularly apathetic in this direction. It is not without meaning that voluntary movement in our country is stronger in those states that are relatively more modernised. The tools of technology, science and management may be brought to bear upon this social movement to usher us towards an integrated and progressive level of modernization.

Chapter 4

Contemporary Social 'Crisis' and its Dimensions

Is there indeed a social crisis in India today? Most people would answer it in the affirmative. The social and psychological igredients of what social scientists define as crisis exist in the contemporary Indian society, e.g. perceptions of generalised social and cultural anomie, an acute sense of disorientation both among the intelligentia and the public, unintended structural shifts and imbalances in society rendering older paradigms of national development open to doubts or even total rejection by some and the breakdown in the national consensus on social and cultural design of society.

In substantive terms, crisis could be segmentary or all-encompassing; it could also be of shorter or longer duration. The segmentary and short-term social crisis could be resolved without major social structural transformation in society. It could also be contained by drawing upon the internal resources of the society. But the all-encompassing crisis of longer duration calls for major structural changes in society. It involves intricate nature of mobilisation both of internal and external resources. A compounding issue in the contemporary social and cultural crisis in India is that here we encounter crises of both segmentary short-term dimensions as well as all-encompassing ones of longer duration.

From Karl Mannheim to Habermas, the European thinkers have been analysing the roots of social and cultural crisis in their society. One may draw some historical lessons from such experiences or even some parallels, but the historicity of the Indian situation calls for caution in theoretic formulation of the issues concerned. For instance, the structural shift from feudalism to capitalism through industrial revolution, the cultural linkages or continuities between rennaissance rationalism and the Calvinistic reformation, the rise of the middle classes with its moulds of right-wing authoritarianism on the one hand and the liberal democratic tradition on the other in Europe, are some historical tendencies which on a surface level might seem to have a parallel with parts of the contemporary social situation in India. One can also postulate a broader relationship between the historical processes of social transformation in society, its class character and the ascendance of the specific types of ideologies.

Historicity of the Indian situation, however, makes it imperative for us to search for specific causes for social and cultural crisis much beyond the factors that may have a universal comparative character. It is obvious that contemporary crisis in our society does not conform to a single pattern. It emanates itself through people's perception of institutional decadence in society, from the increasing disenchantment from the notions of nationalism and national ideology of development. There is growing marginality on this issue among the intellectuals and the elite. Different *competing* ideologies of development and political culture have emerged. The nature of these ideologies remains, however, fuzzy.

The ideology of nationalism and development experienced a historical fracture in India due to the partition of the country on communal lines. It was heroic and far-sighted on the part of our national leadership to have adhered to its chosen path of nationalism aiming at secular, democratic and socialist development of society despite this trauma of history. The Constitution of India reflects this resolve not only by encoding the normative principles but also the agenda of national development. In large measure it also represents the spirit of consensus of the people of India. This consensus continues even today despite some voices of dissent. The voices of dissent existed also in-the past, but today they have assumed menacing proportion with threatening operational strategies. For instance, violence is employed increasingly for realisation of goals. Demands of ethnic identities are converted into open challenge to the legitimacy Of the Constitution. Mobilization by political parties makes open uses of casteism, communalism and regionalism, etc. Political behaviour of most mainline political parties has gained in India today a farcical dimension. The people understand the irony of such behaviour from political leadership; they have over a period of time learnt to laugh at it. But at the hustings they continue to be largely swayed by considerations of caste, region, religion and language, etc. Why is it so? What compulsions motivate people to do so? Is this dissonance between ideology and practice manifestation of the deeper *theme* of the Indian culture which has over the years cultivated a masterly strategy to survive with contradictions!

The crisis in contemporary India invites our attention. to analyse some of these issues. It could probably be understood if we examine the course of social change during the past four and a half decades. Historically, the imminence of crisis or even breakdown of the system is not entirely a new prognosis. Ronald Segal, Selig Harrison, Gunnar, Myrdal, Immanuel Wallerstein, etc. have not only been talking of crisis in India but also making pessimistic predictions about its future. This continued from the middle of the 1950's to the end of the decade of the 1970's. From the 1980's onwards we also begin to come across analytical and empirical writings on India which take note of the positive sides of the development in the society. V.S. Napaul, symbolises this Change in perception. Far from his characterisation of India in the 1950's as an *Area of Darkness* or as a *Wounded Civilization* he now talks of India as a land of a *Million Mutinies,* a symbolization which inheres both despair and hope: Rudolph and Rudoph's *In Persuit of Lakshami* not only takes note of the 'demand politics' but also recognizes the new material gains and the rising aspirations of the people of India. There is indeed a crisis in our society but it has also new qualitative dimensions.

Dimensions of Social Crisis

The dimensions of social crisis that India encountered through 1950's to 1960's in specific areas included acute scarcity of foodgrains and stagnation in agriculture, endemic regional and linguistic tensions in various parts of the country, continuous pressure of population growth burdening the economic, social and human resources and a very low base of industry. The continual conflict with China contributed to the crisis, To take the country beyond stagnation and to achieve the goal of a modern democratic society, the strategy of planned development was adopted.

This strategy derived inspiration from our national movement for independence. Even though planning as an operational tool did bear some influence of the Soviet experience, its social, economic and cultural goals were set by the Indian history and the tradition of national movement. Jawaharlal Nehru, the architect of the process of national development, symbolised the integrated spirit of this renaissance: he was not only influenced by the European industrial revolution and march of its science and technology which helped it to grow into a global imperial power but he was also deeply moved by the liberal socialist humanism as a corrective to ruthless industrial capitalism and its exploitative character. Towering overall, these experiences was the deeper influence upon him of-Mahatma Gandhi who moved his mind and his outlook towards the Indian society and its tradition.

Abolition of the feudal agrarian system, introduction of industrial and scientific renaissance, establishment of an egalitarian welfare society, liberal democracy with secular ideology were set by Nehru as some of the basic goals of planning in India. Following the Gandhian philosophy, means were as important for the achievement of these goals as were the ends: the means being consensual, legal and democratic in design. There has been progress in achieving some goals but many other objectives have yet to be realised

Today, the crisis has assumed a threatening proportion on two major counts: first due to the social and economic character of our achievements resulting from planned change. Secondly, due to non-achievement of our objectives in the crucial sectors of economy and the socio-cultural life. Moreover, there are also some unitended consequences of change emanating both from internal and external factors which every society has to cope up with in the process of social transformation.

Crisis of Achievement

What has India achieved since independence? In answer to this question there is much to be counted: major changes in social structure of society and its system of authority were introduced by abolition of the feudal systems of zamindari, jagirdari and the princely states. It revolutionised the social and the economic base of our rural society whose results now can be seen all over in India's villages. The liberated tenantry has how emerged as the powerful rural middle class. It commands a major voice in the political domain. Largely, the green revolution in the country has been a contribution of this class. The traditions of hard work, social and cultural resilience, tolerant indifference towards Brahamanical tradition, continual involvement in cultural and agrarian movements and pugnacious utilitarianism endows this class today with a major role in the country's social and economic development. Within the caste hierarchy this group occupies the middle space, and today leads the powerful backward-class movement.

Over the past forty-five years, the nation has achieved credible developments in establishing a sound foundation of industrial, technological-scientific and managerial growth. A very substantial technological and scientific manpower has been created. A new middle class quite different in character from the middle classes of the early twentieth century has emerged; it has a much broader social base coming as it does from the middle and lower middle castes and social strata of society. The new entrepreneurs and professional classes in the urban areas and the rich peasantry in villages constitute a middle class in India estimated to be around one fourth of its total population. There has been progressive increase in the percentage of the service sector in the GDP of the country which indicates the extent of change in the economic structure and class composition of society. Colonialism had totally emaciated the industrial foundation of the society, and following independence the country today ranks about thirteenth in terms of industrial advancement. India has reached high degree of excellence in scientific, managerial and technological, education. These achievements have resulted from planned development of society in the basic sectors of its life.

Yet another realm in which success can be attributed to the people of India is that of commitment to liberal democratic polity. Despite a very short abberation during the 'emergency', the country has been able to maintain a vigorous participatory culture of democracy. This has been so despite India ranking quite low in terms of, many pre-requisites of western democratic culture and polity. Looking back, the historical depth of Indian civilization to which the people of India are consciously and unconsciously linked has helped them maintaining the democratic traditions even though forty percent of them are illiterate. Secondly, the traditional institution of 'panchyat' at the levels both of caste and community could be held responsible for inculcating among people a native spirit of democratic interaction and participation. There may be problems in Indian democracy in respect of its legitimation norms, such as the use of caste, religion and region or use of money and muscle power to secure votes, but the fact that democracy has been institutionalised can hardly be disputed. From its fragile base since the early years of independence the continuation of democracy should be taken as a major indicator of social development of the Indian society.

There are many other indicators of development, such as the progressive rise in life expectancy of people, growth in literacy rate, decline in the incidence of child mortality and media exposure of the people. But on each of these indicators for the same time duration other developing countries have done far better than India. In comparison with not only the pacific countries such as South Korea, Taiwan, Indonesia, Malaisya etc. but its immediate neighbours such as Sri Lanka and Pakistan, India ranks lower in economic performance. The contemporary crisis in India, therefore, has its roots both in the nature of its achievements and also lack of growth in the crucial areas of its social and economic life.

Crisis of Failures

As we mentioned above, positive developments have taken place in India since independence. Yet, forty percent of the population is still below the poverty line, and a substantial part of it suffers from destitution. The poor come largely from the scheduled castes and tribes and are concentrated in villages. Due to the policy of reservation in education, government offices and in political representation, etc., a minor section from among these people has risen up to middle class economic status but remains a victim of social and cultural discrimination. The pace of development has created both a psychological and social hiatus between these caste groups and the upper castes in the rural society. Traditionally, the relationship between the deprived or *dalit* castes and the upper and middle castes was that of exploitation through patronage; but following independence due to high degree of politicization, communication exposure and social awareness the *dalits* now not only reject and resent the patronage of the upper-middle castes but also maintain a hostile competitive relationship with them.

In the rural areas the conflict between the two groups has increased. In the States like Bihar, Andhra Pradesh, Madhya Pradesh and pockets of other States of the country this conflictual relationship has taken the form of violent movements such as 'naxalism', 'peoples war group', etc. The tribal population has also shown similar tensions, and has made separatist demands or calls for territorial demarcation for themselves with substantial autonomy. Some demands have already been conceded such as the accord with the Nagas and the Mizos in the Northeast, and the establishment of Gorkhaland in West Bengal with regional autonomy. The talk with the tribes of Chotanagpur region for a Jharkhand state is going on. The Bodos in Assam are also demanding autonomy for themselves. Such demands are, however, not confined to the tribal groups alone. There has been a violent movement going on in Punjab for a separate Khalistan state since the past several years. In Assam a similar movement employing violence goes on.

In large measures (with few exceptions) the conflict between the caste and classes as also the demand for separation or autonomy are related to structural changes in society caused by the social and economic changes since independence. The rise of a new middle class among these groups seems to hold the key to such processes: It is in turn related to the character of the social development in society in which the state has played an instrumental role through planning. Some changes have been in the anticipated direction but a large part of these changes could not have been anticipated.

In the rural areas, the planned effort for development contributed to green revolution. It was led by traditional peasant castes throughout the country who rose to power both political and economic. In comparison with the upper castes who used to be their landlords before independence they still feel culturally and educationally deprived. Hence their movement for reservations for the socially and educationally backward classes in the central services. They already enjoy reservation in most state government jobs and have reservations in educational institutions in the States. This ascendant rural middle class has today a relationship of competitive rivalry with the upper castes. With the *dalits* it maintains a relationship of expl9itative domination. With the rising *dalit* selfawareness there is rising incidence of violence in many parts of the country between these two groups. As the dalits and other poorer sections of the rural society feel more insecure there is rising incidence of migration to cities in search -of jobs. This on the one hand, contributes to imbalanced urbanization (increasing ghettoisation of cities, particularly the metropolises) and on the other, increases the rural c1ass-caste conflict. The conflict results from rebound effect of urbanisation of the rural poor. The pattern or urban migration today is such that linkages of the migrants with the rural economy and society are (unlike in Latin America) not broken. Caste and kinship linkages play a very crucial role in migrants' settlement in urban slums; not only they earn better wages working in cities, particularly with the unorganised sector but they also undergo a great deal of exposure to political education, habituation to urban style consumerism and leisure and enhanced aspiration to move upward in life. It is not uncommon in many cases where these migrant groups accumulate their savings to raise assets in their rural homeland by building houses or purchasing land. The sale of land (particularly in Northern India) is done by upper caste pauperised families who have not been able to adjust with new economic and social changes or it is resorted to by such urban migrants who want to sever their links with the village.

What we wish to highlight through this analysis is the emerging new context of relationships among castes and classes in rural India. Traditional feudal style patronage and exploitation relationships of the past is increasingly being replaced by relationships of conflict and competition. The crisis is that villages have not been able to evolve a new institutional framework through which the changing relationships could be integrated. The villages in India have ceased to be social communities that they once were. They have been transformed into political community, but without an institutional set-up whose legitimacy all groups could recognise.

There is widespread and deeper sense of delegitimation about the state-sponsored institutions. It reinforces the feeling of alienation of people with the state. It portends a deeper crisis which is structurally induced but is often used by some sections as ideologies of separatism, terrorism and violence. It contributes to disenchantment among a section of society not only from the institutional structures but also from the ideology of nation-state and the model of development of society. Why is it so? Which processes of change have brought it about?

The changing perception of the state on the one hand and on the other new structural and ideological changes in society might seem to have induced these contradictions. Both the Constitution and the planning ideology of the state have rested on the principles of social justice, egalitarianism or socialistic pattern of society. Universalisation of primary level education and removal of illiteracy were given a place of prominence in the 'directive principle's of state policy' in the Constitution. Efforts in these directions of change have at the most been half-hearted and halting. Even today about half of the population remains illiterate; among the womenfolk in some states, illiteracy is upto ninety percent. Only in Kerala and a few districts in some states and union territories has the total literacy been achieved. It is discovered that the benefits of the egalitarian policies of the state reach the target groups more effectively and bring more potent results if such groups have education. The education of the girl even upto the seventh standard renders acceptance of the small family norm most effective as is evident in Kerala. It improves health and hygiene, contributes to decline in school dropout rate of children (endemic among the poor) and the more effective uses of the benefits of state resources. It also contributes to enhancement of the entrepreneurial ability of the family as a whole.

But removal of illiteracy has been one major area where we witness monumental failure. Non-accomplishment in tackling the problem of illiteracy and universalisation of education bear organic relationship with failures in the domains of population and health policies. Control of population holds key to most problems that have reached the dimension of crisis in India such as the social structural issues of distributive justice, unemployment, pressure on infrastructures and other related development goals. The figures of 1991 census do not indicate optimism on this count. The rate of population growth is lower in states where standards of education and organised voluntary efforts in implementing state programmes are higher, but this rate (of population growth) is much higher in the less states like Uttar Pradesh, Madhya Pradesh, Rajasthan and

Bihar which together account for the bulk of the country's population. Interestingly, these are also the states which rate poorly on most indicators of development having high degree of poverty, lower productivity in agriculture, high rate of illiteracy, poor indigenous mobilisation of voluntary bodies for development and endemic problems of social unrest and violence. This pattern of what Gunnar Myrdal called 'cumulative causation' in the process of under-development has to be re-orientated through planned investment in crucial sectors, such as the economy, education and infrastructures.

The higher rate of population growth with numerous implications to the gathering crisis in our society and economy bears closer relationship with inter class-caste tensions. With the rise of middle (caste) peasantry to power in villages, the conflict between them and the *dalits* on the one hand and between the *dalits* and the upper caste-class groups on the other has intensified, generally in the self-same states such as Bihar, U.P and parts of Madhya Pradesh etc. where the incidence of poverty and population growth is higher. Similar process could also be observed in other parts of India having similar structural conditions. The push from rural areas due to these structural conditions further generates the urban crisis.

The urban growth in our country follows a curious pattern; it is highest in the metropolitan cities and correspondingly declines as we move from the capital towns to smaller cities and towns. It -only indicates that employment generating activities in the informal sector are highest in metropolitan urban centres and capital towns and lower in other urban centres. This is breeding a serious structural cleavage since it contributes to increasing ghettoisation of the metropolitan centres. The consequence is increased urban unrest, violence and crime. The political pressure of the slum dwellers comes into direct conflict with interests of the urban middleclasses with increasing and unbearable pressure upon infrastructures of the city life. Since in India the urban migrants maintain their links with the villages, the inequitous perception of the urban life and the discontent that it generates is carried over to the countryside where it further reinforces social conflict and violence.

The rural and urban social and cultural systems have interacted closely in our country unlike in many other parts of the world since time immemorial. But with the increasing population pressure the balance of relationships is breaking down. In structural terms, it generates conflict and ideologically it engenders disenchantment with the state. The rural-urban poor show disenchantment from state blaming its policies of development as being pro-rich; the middle class also do not empathise with State policies. The rural middle classes see it as being pro-capitalist and the urban middle classes perceive in state welfare policies e.g. the reservation policies a threat to their well-being.

Although there are continuities in cultural and political domains between the rural and the urban middle classes, in the economic realm, there has existed an awning discontinuity. The urban industrial or business classes due to caste specialisation of occupation had a separate existence. Jainism which produced dominant business leadership was alienated from taking to agriculture. No doubt, since independence a substantial section of the political elites have emerged from the rural upper and middle castes-classes, the professional elite of rural origin still come primarily from the rural upper castes. The rural middle castes have gained in political power but lag behind the upper castes in technical and professional occupations or in administrative and managerial services. Hence the demand for reservation for the backward classes. In business and industry both the upper and the middle rural castes-classes have lagged behind as they did not have its traditions since it was caste specialised.

The dependence upon land, for livelihood and maintenance of a middle class standard of life (which qualitatively keeps on undergoing changes due to overall social and cultural changes) puts enormous pressure upon peasant families. In a generation or two even a land holding of a size within the ceiling limit permitted by the state (about 15-18 acres irrigated land) gets fragmented. And without avenues for mobility to non-agricultural employment the younger generation of peasants finds itself exposed to unavoidable downward social mobility or even pauperisation. This may lead to political radicalism or violence. The incidence of farmers accumulating capital and investing their surpluses into business or industry are rare in our country. It has not happened in Punjab where country's first green revolution took place. It has very partially happened in Maharashtra and Gujarat. Some evidence of such transition (from agriculture to business industry) could be found in parts. of Andhra Pradesh where rich farmers, particularly the Kammas and Reddys of the Krishna-Godawari valleys due mainly to cash crop cultivation have slowly moved out towards industrial production graduating through commercial and real estate enterprises. Such mobility is, however, rare. Avenues of employment outside agriculture specially in agro-industries, services, industrial production and professions, etc. are imperative for a healthy development of the agrarian economy and society, even though green revolution might offer us a succour for awhile. Already in our villages, especially among the youth there is total disenchantment from the rural life. Its community life is broken due to over politicisation and caste-class tensions, and its economy is burdened by over-population and structural precariousness. To overcome this problem an integrated plan of rural-urban and agro-industrial development would be required. In its absence, even our green revolution (its shine is already withering due to capital and technology lag) may offer us a momentary relief from the impending future social structural crisis.

The cleavages between the class-caste groups in rural society have their parallels in the urban-industrial sector as well. We have already drawn attention to urbanward migration from villages which has serious consequences. The estimates of the National Commission on Urbanization are disquieting indeed. By the second quarter of the twenty-first century India's population is likely to cross one billion mark (out-stripping that of China) and its pressure on the urban centres, (metropolitan ones particularly) would be unbearable. Our rural crisis is most likely to be compounded with a large urban crisis already in the making.

Cultural Crisis in the Process of Change

We have so far discussed some dimensions of crisis arising out of the process of social structural mobility and change. The cultural consequences of these changes too are not system-integrative. The new rural middle classes and urban professionals and entrepreneurial groups have shown capacity for initiative and innovation. It has, however, been accompanied by a sharp decline in the values of social responsibility, social welfarism and personal asceticism (values which inspired our freedom movement led by Gandhiji). Unlike in Europe the new entrepreneurial and professional classes are not inspired by values of puritan ethic or by consumer-nationalism as in Japan.

The uses of connections, of family and kinship, of regions and language and of political leaders and bureaucracy have been central to the Indian entrepreneurs' success in business and industry. Structurally it has often foreclosed the entry of new entrepreneurs to business but it has also maintained a continuity of tradition in the process of economic modernisation of society. Its most vitiating consequence, however, has been the misuse of the "political" connections which under a controlled economy regime did build up a large number of business families but at the same time delegitimised ethical norms. The state being the sponsor of most such opportunities, helped in creation of a cultural ethos which is, on the one hand alienative in respect of state-public relationship, and on the other breeds a strong dependency syndrome. This process of cultural dis-orientation has bred an unprincipled go-getter utilitarianism which today pervades through business, profession, politics and education and governs the value system of the new rural and urban middle classes. Corruption in public life and. cynicism in ideology are its logical result.

It has deeply affected the work ethic in our society. The state which was rightly brought into the role of establishing welfare through its active economic and social interventions has been mis-perceived as an institution that rewards manipulators, is permissive and offers enormous scope for quick upward mobility through corrupt appropriation of public resources and wealth. It has reinforced "jobism" and not a work ethic. The demand for government jobs as distinct from 'opportunity to work' is a result of this process. Reservation of jobs for the socially and economically deprived sections of our society has been a right policy intended to repair the balance of forces that handicapped them since centuries. But it has now been, or is now most likely to be converted into a hereditary privilege.

Such developments have brought into being an ideological chaos in India without the end of ideology. Ideologies still survive and are competing for domination. Mention may be made of two crucial ideologies which also reflect the crisis that India faces today. These are ideologies of *nationalism* and *communalism.* Both have a long historical past in our freedom movement. The ideology of nationalism got. flawed by the trauma of partition but it survived. But communalism poses a serious threat to this ideology. Communalism in its narrow sense of conflict and intolerance among religious groups, particularly the Hindus and the

Muslims is often orchestrated by social forces and groups (new rural-urban middle classes) whose rise in society we have examined. Communal violence erupts recurrently as apotheosis of ethically rootless economism here or a political opportunism there. It is anchored not in commitment to religious values, which have maintained a tradition of pluralism and tolerance in India through ages, a spirit which has not yet fully declined. Communalism thrives on the exploitation of deprivation anxiety. As such, it could possibly be contained through judicious administration of policies of egalitarianism and social welfare in favour of the deprived groups among the religious minorities.

Communalism poses threat to India in yet a vital sense where it counterposes itself against nationalism. Being a plural society with its divisions based on caste, religion, language, ethnicity and region, etc., bonds of unity in India have always been provided by diffuse and flexible sharing of certain common values, occupational skills, technologies, artifacts and market relationships despite differences of religion, language or region. This we could characterise as 'civilisational' unity of India as different from a nation-state. That is why through millenia India remained a land where people of all faiths, of cultural and linguistic diversities could live together in harmony. The rulers of India coming from different religious background respected and fostered this tradition, It provided for enormous regional autonomy with varying degrees of central control. Some historical and anthropological evidence suggests that degree of centralisation increased with the coming of the Mughal rule and went on increasing during the British regime. The British colonial regime and its institutional innovations had an effect that spurred the ideology of a nation-state deriving substantial inspiration from the west. Despite this, the Constitution of India is a unique document, tilting more towards centralisation though with enough flexibility for decentralisation of power.

The normative structure of nationalism that the Constitution projects is of a state that is secular; socialist, democratic and protective of all basic human rights irrespective of birth, religion and gender. The character of social economic development since independence has been such that a consensus on its operational strategies and premises has today declined. The processes of social mobility have sharpened the conflicts but the cleavages are not yet crystallised on class lines. These cut across divisions on the basis of caste, class and religion.

Under this milieu the growth of middle classes in both the Hindu and the Muslims communities has created an articulate support base for propagation of communal ideology. In recent times this development has given fillip to political parties and caucuses openly legitimising communalism. The erosion in the influence of the Congress party, the rising wave of Islamic fundamentalism in the muslim countries, interpreted by Hindu and Muslim communalists out of the context, sharpens communal prejudices. This face of communalism has, structurally speaking, more enduring and fearsome implications. It is not based on short run passions which erupt into communal violence orchestrated by vested interests it has deeper and wider implications. It poses a threat to the notion of civilisation which Indian tradition fostered since, millenia—one of pluralism and heteronomy, that is tolerance for all religious faiths and styles of living. Partly, religious fundamentalism manifests oriental disillusionment with the western model of modernisation.

The religious orientation takes a communal form when it is politicised and starts setting down rules for nationalism and economic and social development. Without offering clarity on how such ideology would cope up with issues of a modern secular-democratic state, its response is only hazy. Communalism of this variety could be most threatening for India which is still in the process of making itself into a nation-state. A nation is not a state of being like a finished architecture, but a process of becoming. Religious fundamentalism in its communal manifestation can be disruptive for this process of becoming a secular nation-state.

Social Crisis and Paths of Development

One may be tempted to attribute much of this crisis to our chosen path of development since independence. To us this appears to be flawed if not fallacious. Development is not a linear but a retroactive process, and considering our options and limitations of social structure and its historicity, the planning model with state initiative has I been the best choice. Sustainability is an issue which emerges historically; it is so in the west, and we should look at it with a sense of history. Some lessons from the history of planning are already evident, such as relevance of decentralisation, of involvement of the people and the voluntary groups in the development process, crucial role of education in development (specially education of women and removal of illiteracy), the need for integrated rural-urban planning, the improvement of infrastructures and eco-friendly industrialisation. The need to create job opportunities in villages and small towns and the urgency to improve their quality of life is now widely recognised too. But most these innovations are organic to the planning process as envisaged. The new challenge to its basic direction and philosophy, however, have come from recent policy changes towards market-friendly approach.

In a survey *The Economist* (May 4th 1991) has characterised the Indian state controlled economy and its goal of self-sufficiency as the main hurdle to its growth. On most economic indicators such as real agricultural output, average annual increase in the volume of industrial output, average annual reduction in poverty and under-five (years) mortality rate, and even on goals of self reliance assessed in terms of export-import performance, the Indian economy has lagged behind almost all other Asian countries. Because of the statist policies according to this survey the fuller blossoming of the Indian economic potential has not been realised. India is like a tiger in a cage. In an earlier survey (*The Economist,* November 16th 1991) the process of economic growth at a very rapid rate in the economies of the East and South-East Asian countries has been attributed to their market-friendly open economies. Summing up the fundamental lessons of these economies the survey states: "the priority of state action should be economic. development, defined not by the government's ability to hand out welfare payments to the less privileged, but rather by growth in output, productivity and above all, international, competitiveness; rapid growth is impossible without a commitment to markets and private property.... Markets do not have to be completely free and relatively equal distribution of incomes and relatively low taxes motivate workers" (*The Economist,* November 16th 1991).

This analytical reasoning coinciding with changes in the global situation has created a massive, often unthinking support for an open, capitalist, market-friendly economic policy coinciding with a democratic polity throughout the world. India has recently undertaken a cautious shift in many of its economic policies in this direction. It has correctly been realised that the extension of state in the sphere of economic activities such as trade and industry beyond a point breeds inefficiency and corruption. State sector of production becomes non-competitive and a protected capitalism thrives at the cost of the people. Therefore, economic liberalisation and its global market I linkages are necessary not -only for more efficiency but also for technological advancement for higher volume and quality of production. Lagging behind such support even our green revolution is now faced with stagnation. But there are limits to this policy.

The developing countries like India must take into

account their own historicity on such issues in accordance with the limits that our social structure, values and political order impose upon such policies. Even in the developed Europe there is a rethinking among some intellectuals. Pierre Boaurdieu, a leading European sociologist, has this to say about the prevailing dominance of market economic rationality and individualism in France: "Blinkered as they are by narrow, short-sighted IMF-inspired economic theory—which is wreaking havoc in North-South relations and will continue to do so—these half baked economists naturally forget to take into account the actual short-term, and above all long-term, cost of the financial and moral misery that is the only certain outcome of economically legitimised realpolitik: delinquency, criminality, alcoholism, road accidents and so on" (interview in *Le Monde,* translated and reproduced in *Gaurdian Weekly,* February 2, 1992).

Bourdieu addresses himself to the European context. In our own context the policy of economic liberalisation would have to be evolved to suit our social and political conditions. Democracy itself brings constraints to reform processes even when desirable, and its foreplay would have to be orchestrated with social responsibility and human conscience. This would mean emphasis on equality and distributive justice for the weaker sections of society. The protective wings of social welfarism with suitable incentives to individual initiative and capacity for production would have to be maintained in the economic reform policy of the coming several years in India. It does not involve obsolescence of Gandhi-Nehru model of social and economic development but only its innovative exegesis in the changing social and economic environment of the world.

REFERENCES

1. Bouddieu Pierre, in *Guardian Weekly,* February 2, 1992.
2. *The Economist,* May 4, 1991.
3. *The Economist,* November 16, 1991.

Chapter 5

Economic Development and the Changing Family System

The relationship between economic development and changes in the family system have been studied by anthropologists, sociologists and historians. In India, several studies have reported close association between changes in economy, emerging entrepreneurial structures and processes of change in the family system. Similarly, studies have also delineated the relationship between family systems and their impact on the nature and direction of economic development. Much speculation persists whether traditional societies at pre-industrial level of economic development with everwhelming base of joint family systems could successfully accomplish industrial development and modernization. Some Marxist historians and economists have postulated a weakening of relationship between family system and family mode of production with the rise of capitalism. A dissociation between family system and modern industrial mode of production is assumed, and contrariwise it is believed that nuclearization of family system may be a universal process in the industrial pattern of economy. A general assumption has prevailed that industrial economy must essentially imply the decline of all traditional communitarian institutions such as joint family, caste and community and religious beliefs and styles of life.

The studies on the processes of industrial development in India have revealed that most these assumptions are not universally valid, and do not apply to the Indian situation. Most often, such assumptions are based on historically specific instances which do not apply to other societies. The nuclearisation of family structure as an essential and universal consequence of changes following industrialisation is held as valid by a number of sociologists and social anthropologists (see, Moore W.E: 1965 Goode: 1963 etc.). Yet, the evidence from the Western Societies suggested that rather than industrialisation being a cause of widening nuclear family pattern the latter may be a result of pre-existing nuclear family system- in society. Comparative analyses of family systems and their role in economic modernization do not support the nuclearization of family as a universal process.

Industrialization, Entrepreneurship and Family Systems

An important aspect in the treatment of the Indian and some other developing societies by the Western social scientists is the assumption that traditionalism in the social structure of these societies, such as family jointness, extended kinship bonds and caste and community cleavages would not be conducive for industrial and cultural modernization. It is also believed that as processes of economic modernization gain momentum, the traditional institutions, the joint family system, etc. would give ground to modern forms, e.g. the nuclear family system. Studies on the relationship between industrial entrepreneurial development and the family systems in India question the validity of these propositions. There is enough evidence adduced by economists, sociologists and social anthropologists to suggest that processes of industrial and entrepreneurial growth in India have received support from the joint family system. The studies which postulate that industrial and economic modernization would lead to nuclearization of family systems (Ross A: 1961; Gore M.S: 1968 and Davis K: 1958) are often based not on systematic structural study of family system but on attitudinal data, A. time-depth analysis of family system over successive generations by J.P. Desai revealed a cyclical rather than a linear movement from jointness to nuclearity (Desai I.P.: 1964).

No doubt, industrial and urban developments in India are contributing to changes in many rules of jointness in the family system, such as rules of residence, forms of marriage and authority system. But these changes are adaptive in character. Rule of residence is of prime significance for changes in family structure resulting from industrial and urban growth. Murdock rightly opines: "It is in respect to residence that changes in economy, technology, property, government, or religion first alter the structural relationships of related individuals to one another, giving an impetus to subsequent modifications in forms of the family, in consanguineal and compromise kin groups, and in kinship terminology" (Murdock G.P: 1949:202). Migration to cities and towns for work has increased during the past decades, and depending upon the nature of work it affects the joint family system. Also migration from villages to cities and from one city to another for technical and professional occupations results into setting up of nuclear families comprising husband, wife and children, occasionally aged mother or father is invited to live or nieces and nephews may be resident for education. In most such cases, the form that family takes is that of supplemented nuclear family. Even in nuclear families, nuclearity is only residential and functionally the joint family obligations in performance of rituals, kinship and marriage obligations and in ownership of assets and properties and sharing of economic responsibilities are maintained. Those who migrate to cities from rural areas seeking jobs in informal sectors of economy, the pattern is collective and rarely individual. Several members of the joint family including wife, children and brothers, etc. migrate. Earlier, mainly the male members of the joint family migrated to cities for work. This continues but the new tendency is of family migration to cities for work. This results into urban slums and hutments where families of workers establish settlements and continue with traditional family obligations, rituals, values and beliefs.

There are many other ways in which industrialization, urbanisation and diversification of occupations have affected the family systems in India. Differentiation in occupational structure, increase in education of women and urbanization have changed the pattern of mobility, the character of jointness in the family in terms of residence, kinship relationship and social and economic ties. The studies on regional variations ill family patterns in India by Pauline Kolenda can indirectly be treated as indicators of the emerging relationship between economic development, caste and joint family structures. Kolenda, based on twenty-six studies on family systems in rural and urban India writes: "while these studies suggest that most Indians do not live in joint families, as defined here, they do suggest that most (rural people at least) live in either a joint or a supplemented nuclear family. While the majority of people may live in such joint and supplemented nuclear families, the majority of families defined here as commensal units, are probably nuclear in structure. Emerging during the research were other hypotheses. First, there appear to be regional differences in proportion of joint families. It may be that there are higher proportions of joint families on the Gangetic Plain than in Central India (represented by studies in Maharashtra, Madhya Pradesh, and Western Rajasthan), or in West Bengal. There may be higher proportions of joint families among most castes in north western Mysore state. There also appear to be places such as Gokak Taluk, Belgaum District, Mysore, in which all castes appear to have higher proportions of joint families, and places such as Badlapur, Thana District Maharashtra, where almost all local caste groups have low proportions of joint families" (Kolenda P: 1987:77-78). Using a statistical analysis of census data Kolenda and Lorraine Haddon offer further confirmation of regional variations in family patterns.

There is no direct evidence in these regional variations which could correlate with levels or patterns of economic development, such as industrialization and urbanization. But the data do suggest joint family being more frequent in agricultural, upper and middle caste groups and supplemented nuclear family among the urban professional and business classes. If one combines the frequency of joint family households with supplemented nuclear families, which only manifest a variation on the joint family systems, the dominant family structure in India tends to be that of the joint and not of the nuclear family system. Its economic correlates are substantial.

The process of economic development has a variable impact on the family systems. Urbanization and industrialization have no doubt led to some breakdown in the traditional joint family and have contributed to the growth of supplemented and other varieties of nuclear families. Apart from the general growth in education, the education of women in India has increased substantially during the past decades. It has increased the chances of their professional employment. Women's enrolment of university education (all faculties) doubled during 1950-51 and 1970-71. Their employment in professions, especially teaching has also more than doubled during the same period (see, ICSSR: 1975). By categories of employment ironically in non-skilled and semi-skilled categories the share of women has gone down. Their share of employment in factories and organised public or private sector industries has also declined. It fell from 11.43 per cent in factory employment in 1951 to 9.1 per cent in 1971. In public and private sector organized sector the women's employment level was 65 per cent in 1962; it went down to 52.8 per cent in 1973. This uneven pattern of growth in women's employment indicates tensions of modernization in economic technological and educational fields which India has been experiencing. Whereas the rise in higher education of women has increased their share in professional and service sector jobs, the technological advancements in mining, factory production and other industrial sectors including agriculture has had a negative effect on their employment. The impact that it has on the family system in India can only be hypothesised in the absence of systematic studies. It has meant urban-ward migration of couples in nuclear or supplemented nuclear family settings. It may have also increased numerically the single member family units in cities, especially of working men and women, migrating from outside. The educational, technological and industrial advancement and growth in professional, organised sector skilled jobs and other ancillary services have had many consequences for the family system which are as yet transitional. These do not seem to have caused a breakdown in the joint family bonds, and yet these promote a variety of forms of nuclearity. Culturally, given the strong caste, community and kinship ties in India, the culture of joint family system continues to prevail.

This is evident from a study that Michael M. Ames conducted on the factory workers in the Steel City of Jamshedpur to measure their ideal family preferences. He reports: "The large majority of respondents in the subsample quite clearly consider the traditional single residence joint family as the most respectable, honourable, or "ideal" type of family to maintain, even if they do not themselves have such family or consider one now possible". For example, a proposition that—"if it is possible then people should live together in a joint family"—is accepted strongly or moderately by almost 91 per cent of the respondents, even though in reference to their *own* particular families only half the respondents prefer common residence" (Ames M.M.: in Milton singer: 1973:123). This confirms the variable impact that industrialization has upon the family systems. It is mediated by "a number of factors, such as education, income, caste, ethnicity, which themselves may vary independently of industrialization". Similarly, "the several concrete dimensions of family structure may "respond" differently to the pressure of an industrial environment ... The residential dimension, where the worker lives, is of course, closely related to, or interdependent with, the man's occupation; it is therefore hardly surprising that residential practices should reflect occupational pressures. Property ownership, on the other hand, is susceptible to pressures that range far more widely in both space and time" (Ames: 1973: 125). The patterns of change is such that the joint family norm continues to ideologically dominate.

Apart from the impact that industrialization has upon the family system, the latter also influences the nature and direction of industrial and economic growth in societies. This has been brought out by several Indian studies dealing with social correlates of industrialization and entrepreneurship. The early studies demonstrated the role of joint families and traditional caste occupations in the rise of business classes, capital formation and the nature of industrial management. The joint business families contributed to the establishment of textile mills, steel factories and other industrial entreprises apart from trade and banking as noted by economists and historians (see, Gadgil D.R: 1959; Mehta S.D: 1953). In early phases of industrial entrepreneurship these families played a role in mobilization of capital, procurement of managerial and technical skills and in establishing marketing networks. Recently, the relationship between family structure and the emergence of business enterprises has been the subject of many studies. The caste, community and religious backgrounds of the successful entrepreneurs in addition to their family structure have been analysed.

The focus of these studies varies, but all of them deal

with the interface between industrial enterprise and family systems. First type of studies deals generally with the role of caste and community in the rise of modern capitalist entrepreneurship and show its relationship with traditional family occupations to explain the success in this domain (Fox R.C: 1973; Mines M: 1973; in Singer M: 1973; Timberg T.A: 1978; Singer M: 1960, 1968; 1972; Shoji Ito: 1966; Sujata K: 1982). These studies analyse the nature of institutions such as joint family, occupational traditions and kinship and community ties either in a single business caste or community or study interaction of these factors with the successes achieved in industrial enterprises. Some studies also attempt to explore how traditional occupation and joint family system of these groups contributed to their evolution from small traders to pariah capitalists and finally into big industrial entrepreneurs. An important common ground covered in most these studies is to establish a continuity between modern business aptitudes and traditional roles and values related to family, kinship, community and caste, etc.

The second type of studies, though fewer, examine the relationship between family system and organization of industrial firms in the context of modernization of management, distribution of authority and inter-generational relationships. Consolidation of family firms and expansion in their business through marital ties constitutes an important aspect of these studies (see, Sujata K: 1982; Timberg: 1978; Spodek: 1965). Finally, there are studies which analyse transitional processes of movement from agricultural to commercial-industrial enterprises as a result of economic development (Ownes R: 1973; Marriott M: 1973). In these studies aspects of social mobility and the emerging technological and entrepreneurial orientation among the peasantry have been analysed. These bear relationship with the family system not directly but by inference since most wealthy peasants having extended or joint families generate agricultural surpluses working through a family mode of production. This· mode of production generates surpluses that are made available for investment in business and industrial enterprises as also for education which adds to their ability for social mobility.

The relationship between economic development and family system dealing with changes in the authority structure in the family such as status withdrawal of heads of household and its consequent impact on personality system of children, a precursor to their growth as innovative personality types associated with innovative entrepreneurial culture and role-sets in society (Hagen E: 1962) which is supposed to have been a prime factor in the modernization of society and economy in the west, has not been deeply studied in India. Very few studies of the industrial entrepreneurs have dealt with their cultural and social modernization through changes in their personality system brought about by crisis in the authority structure of their families. One study which comments on this issue while studying industrial entrepreneurs in a Punjab town is critical of the proposition of "status withdrawal". It suggests that what happens more often in case of the entrepreneur families of Punjab is not status withdrawal but "status accrual" through industrial advancement, (see, Saberwal S: 1976). Similarly, McClelland's theory of achievement orientation and successful entrepreneurial behaviour has also been found to be of only marginal relevance in entrepreneurial performance. It is the other factors, especially entrepreneurial environment which govern the success or failure of entrepreneurs in India as revealed by a study of entrepreneurs in Howrah, Calcutta (Nandy A: 1973). On the other hand, Hanna Papaneck considers that "in the Indian context the requirement for a successful entrepreneurial personality include autonomy and personal responsibility. These are supposed to be fostered by a "mother less indulgent than the average and a father who is physically absent or relatively uninvolved in the upbringing of his son" (quoted in Timberg: 1973:25). The significance of these studies lies in the implicit recognition of the role of specific cultural and historical factors in India (as against the universalistic constructs of Hagen and McClelland) in the growth of entrepreneurial personality, its roles and structures. We witness once again the elements of continuity and historicity in the impact that family system has upon the growth of economic and cultural modernization.

The relationship between family system and industrial development is more directly postulated in the studies of business castes, communities and occupational groups. Marwaris in the north and eastern India, Chettiars in the south and Parsis in the western India are examples of caste or community who contributed to the growth of industrial entrepreneurship in India. Their transition from traditional merchants to industrial capitalists has been studied in the contexts of their family; community and ideology. The biographies of the leading entrepreneurs from these communities have also been evaluated. Timberg who studied the rise of the Marwaris to industrial capitalism refers to the role that joint family system played in enabling these traditional traders to become industrial entrepreneurs. He writes: "In connection with their specialization in trade, these communities have developed various institutions which enable them to trade more easily. If wives and children are left at home so that males can travel on business, the joint family home provides shelter for family dependents. Wandering traders find, wherever they go, support and housing provided them by their communal fellows" ... (Timberg: 1978:5). Then with specific reference to the role of joint family in the success of the Marwaris as industrial entrepreneurs Timberg writes:"

> We are thus led to re-examine the functions of traditional commercial and social values and institutions as they are used by trading communities in

the transition to "modern" forms of economic activity. Perhaps it is the presence rather than the absence of these values, which made the Marwaris and some other commercial communities successful. It may be that many institutions, such as the joint family and strong particularistic caste loyalities are the secret of success in Indian business and industry. For example, the retention of the joint family allegedly restrains entrepreneurs. The individual is constrained by the group and cannot move forward. On the other hand, there is strong indication that a joint family may be a useful institution for mobilizing otherwise scarce factors, such as capital" (Timberg: 1978: 17).

Similar conclusions have been drawn by researches on other business communities. Milton Singer (1968) found that traditional joint family among entrepreneurs in Madras played important role in their success through adaptive changes including adjustments in the system of authority, decision-making in the enterprises and in the processes of management. This also covers issues related to training and education of the younger members of the family to take over supervision and management of firms. Compartmentalization of responsibilities and authority tends to be an important strategy of these industrial families. Intensive analysis of adjustments in the structure of industrial families in the process of growth in their enterprises has been conducted by Allan Cohen based on data from eight firms in India. He has observed role-conflict in family business in situations where role pressures of membership of more than one organizations generates incompatabilities and conflicts. The conflict in family firms is greater when there is more emphasis on modernization of the management style. To maintain harmonious relationships within the family firm, according to Cohen adaptive strategies in management styles are adopted (Cohen Allan: 1974). The findings of Cohen under specific circumstances have been confirmed by other studies of family firms in India (see, Sujata K:1982). A combination of factors maintain" the link of modern family firms with tradition. The *Mitakshra* law of inheritance which sanctions joint ownership of property contributes to the unity of family. Also the cultural factors such as ideological preference for joint family as a measure of the ethic of accommodation and reconciliation sanctified by tradition sustains its unity despite tensions and role conflicts in the process of economic modernization. This has been confirmed by a comparative study of three business families one each belonging to the Parsi, the Gujarati and the Marwari community (Sujata K: 1982). Several other studies also support this viewpoint.

Modernization of Agriculture and Family System

Important changes have been taking place in the rural family system since the onset of agricultural modernization. Considering the substantial place that rural society occupies even today in the Indian social system, and the increasing linkages that it is developing with urban and industrial sectors of economy, these changes have a far reaching significance to modernization of society. They are also significant because of the present direction of changes and its challenge as demonstrated by social processes in the structure of the rural family systems. The nuclear families are predominant among the working classes, marginal farmers and lower castes. Pauline Kolenda's study of regional patterning in the family structure shows that "it is least characteristic of local *jatis* of Untouchables. It may be somewhat more characteristic of higher "twice-born" castes"; moreover, she also states "that most (rural people at least) live in either a joint or supplemented nuclear family" (Kolenda P: 1973:87). In caste terms, it would appear that most upper castes have a predominance of joint or supplemented nuclear families, most middle castes with medium to large landholding have joint families and the landless labourers or lower castes mostly live in nuclear families.

This patterning of family structure in rural society has assumed significance in economic development of villages, particularly in modernization of agriculture known as the "green revolution". Small nuclear families of agricultural workers make it possible for them to migrate from less developed agricultural regions such as Bihar, Uttar Pradesh, Orissa, etc. with the entire family to agriculturally developed states such as Punjab, Haryana and Gujarat, ete. The joint family system of the peasant castes has played a very basic role in modernization of their agriculture and their economic prosperity. The investments made in agriculture during the 1950's brought about "green revolution" in agriculture during late 1960's. This triggered new social, political, economic and cultural processes in the countryside. Studies on the social structure of this agricultural modernization reveals that in most regions of India, such as Punjab, Haryana, Western Uttar Pradesh, Gujarat, Maharashtra, etc. the traditional peasant castes contributed predominantly to the green revolution. The Jats in Punjab, Haryana and Western U.P., the Kurmis and Ahirs in pans of Eastern U.P., the Patidars and Kunbis in Gujarat, the Marathas in Maharashtra, the Kammas, Reddys and Vokkaligas in the peninsular India were directly involved in the process of this agricultural modernization. These were also the groups which had substantial landholdings and had taken maximum advantages of land reforms introduced after Independence. They also had a long tradition of cultivation in India and were known for hard work, pragmatic outlook and traditional form of rationality typical of the Indian society.

These agricultural groups had strong joint family system and family mode of work on the farms which involved all members of the household. This probably has been a feature of all peasant societies which had led to much discussion on the "family mode of production" among social scientists (see Banaji J: 1976). Particularly Chayanov's thesis of positive correlation between family size and volume of average production has been a subject for debate. In most peasant castes in India, however, joint family system is a common feature. Studies show that a large size of landholding and a well-knit joint family are the mark of social prestige and bring political power to such families. These factors also reinforce joint family ties. The viability of economic status that joint family farms promote adds to its persistence. The extensive use of family labour (with some additions from outside as the need may be) contributes to the maximization of economic surpluses. This, together with peasant culture of austerity in consumption styles, especially for the women and the junior members in the family, adds to savings and strengthens the economic status of such families.

The green revolution has not only contributed to strengthening the bonds of jointness in the peasant family, it has also introduced economic and technological modernization. There has been a reciprocal reinforcement to a large extent. The technological demands of r:tew agriculture have brought into wake new social conditions in the functioning of the family system. An important change seems to be in the structure of authority and the process of decision making. Traditionally, the elder head of household took decisions in all matters of the family—social, cultural, economic and technological. With modernization of agriculture and its new linkages with administrative and developmental agencies spread far and wide, a change has taken place. The younger educated or semi-educated members in the households look after the most technical and managerial activities of farming, its credit and marketing side, etc., where the actual head of the house-hold plays only a minor role, but is social matters such as marriage rituals, distribution of goods and resources etc., the traditional head of the household continues to play his role. Thus, an adaptive change, which varies from region to region does seem to be taking place in the authority structure of the peasant family system in India.

Changes are taking place in other aspects of the joint family system among the peasantry, not only among the middle but among the upper caste peasants also. The economic development in the villages has brought about some changes in consumption patterns even though there is no association between family size and increase in consumption (Sivakumar S S: 1976). Although as yet only a marginal change in consumption style of the peasant families has taken place, more changes in course of The agricultural development may, however, be anticipated. These will have an impact on the joint family system, especially on its' cohesion and norms of conformity. Studies on the variation of family structure in course of the capitalist development in agriculture in the regions of green revolution establish that processes both of nucleation in some agrarian strata and cohesion of joint family system in others are taking place. The viability of the joint family system, despite capitalist development remains intact because the Indian experience of agrarian capitalism has principally land as asset for investment. Ramkrishana Mukherjee's study of tHe *"West Bengal Family Structure,* 1946-66 also reiterates the viability of joint family system (Mukherjee R.K: 1977). Studying the relationship between agrarian structure and the family formation based on the rate of partitioning of households belonging to different agrarian strata in Kerala, N. Krishnaji finds that despite in some cases nucleation of families in the process of agrarian transition taking place, the joint family system prevails as a dominant form.

Migration may bring about break with the rural parent families in case of the landless households, but this is not the case for the families with land holdings. "This can be expected to be true especially in the case of families owning large land-holdings. In such cases while the family is subdivided in a physical sense, its different branches may continue to invest jointly in activities allied to agriculture and centred round the family holding" (Krishnaji N: 1980:A-39). "In sum, we may hypothesise that nucleation of families, while being associated with capitalist development in general, need not affect all agrarian classes uniformly. The processes of dispossession and pauperization of the peasantry can promote nucleation at one end of the peasant spectrum while consolidating the joint family system (or rather retarding its decay) at the other, especially when ownership of land remains the principal means or acquiring wealth" (Krishnaji K: 1980:A-39). When we read these findings along with the role that the joint family system has played in strengthening the family firms in the industrial sector, we see the continuing significance of the joint family system in the process of Indian economic development. We have already noticed how industrial investment is aided by the joint family system which helps in raising capital, labour and other resources (right connections for getting licences, raw materials and permits, etc.) and contributes to the managerial supervision (Safa H.I: 1982). The same parallel though in a different form also exists in case of the peasant joint family systems.

The developments in the agrarian structure are not uniform and vary from region to region. Therefore, the effect of agrarian development on the family system must show a variety of responses. In Punjab and Haryana social developments resulting from green revolution have generated stresses in the joint family system from accelerating subdivision of family farms. There has been a downward shift in the acreage structure of the operated holdings over the period of a decade. The distribution of operated land and assets has moved in favour of the big farmers (Bhalla S: 1977). Intensive pressure on land due to absence of rural industries has contributed to de-industrialization and increase in the proportion of workers in agriculture (Bhalla S: 1977). All this implies that although joint family might constitute the dominant structure in case of the peasants with big landholdings, the pressure of population in the family leads to structural nucleation despsite the family remaining functionally joint as we found in the case of Kerala. These social stresses of agrarian development have set into motion processes of restructuration in family system and its relationship with economy.

However, green revolution has in most cases reinforced the joint family system which, as in the realm of industry, plays a significant role in economic modernization of the rural economy. There is, however, also a process of nucleation going on, which economists associate with streses resulting from growth of capitalist agriculture. This proposition might sometimes imply the fallacious inference that joint family system is a passing phase in the process of industrialisation. However, the attempt to understand the processes of change in the family system merely through statistical measurements or through structural differentiation in the family system is inadequate for grasping its true dynamics. Milton Singer rightly observes: "it is no longer possible to support conclusions about the breakdown of the joint family by citing statistics on the frequency of nuclear households. The burden of proof has shifted: one must distinguish the cultural ideal of joint family from its actual occurrence, and attitudes and sentiments from behaviour. Different types of joint families (lineal, collateral and others) must be distinguished, as must different types of nuclear families" (Singer M: 1968:425). The scrutiny of *kula-vritanta* or family history among the Chitpavan Brahamans of Maharashtra reveals increasingly "that family organization is felt to be good in itself and to be an end in itself. Within the context of a hostile world, some of the authors seem to be saying that it is comforting to know who one's family members, *kula-bandhu* are, and to watch how they are adjusting to changing circumstances" (Patterson M.L.P.: 1968:409). The strength of the joint family ideology as it confronts the forces of economic modernization shows itself through its adaptive resilience.

Modernization, Economic Development and Family System

The Indian experience of economic modernization and its impact on social structure and cultural values have a historicity of their own. We witness it at many levels of adaptive responses that traditional institutions have made in India in the process of economic, political and cultural modernization. Institutions like caste, religion, joint family system and strong bonds of kinship and community, which many western social scientists held to be obstacles in the path of India's modernization, were found to respond positively to accommodate the forces of modernization. Not that the process of adaptive transformation has been painless or without deviant manifestations. In the system of joint family itself the contradictions between goals and means of rapid economic advancement have led to distorted aspirations and contributed in recent days to rising incidence of demand for dowry in marriages. Many deaths of brides in the event of dowry not being satisfactory or not being paid have been reported. Victimization of women in many other spheres of family, their exploitation by in-laws, husbands and other members of the groom's family is widespread. The rate of divorce though still low in comparison to other countries is rising as more and more women are asserting their legitimate rights. Many women's organisations are engaged in the work of protection of women and restoration of their due rights. These processes demonstrate how the forces of modernization and economic development are tending to generate tensions of restructuration in society. But the over-arching social development remains adaptive and resilient in respect of the transition from tradition to modernization.

This we have found in how the joint family system has contributed to the process of indigenous development of . industrial economy, a transition from traditional mercantile trade to industrial family firms. But we also notice that in the process of evolution of this kind conflicts and tensions have also arisen between the forces of nucleation and jointness in the family structure. This takes place on issues of styles and scope of management, rationalization of firms and on its inheritance and control. But more often, business and industrial families succeed in striking reconciliation Dr balance between principles of primordiality and rationality in control and management. In the field of agrarian modernization we find a similar process taking place. The joint family structure of the peasant households has served as a reservoir of manpower and resources to carry forward agricultural modernization. Both in cases of the family firms and peasant farms changes in the authority structure of the joint family system have taken place without a major break from the traditional values and norms. Even the process of nucleation, which is no doubt going on alongwith reinforcement of the joint family structure at different levels, does not portend a linear process of change from jointness to nuclearity. On the contrary, the dominating cultural framework within which these changes in the family structure are taking place is grounded in the idealization of joint family norms in society. Thus, there are changes but many continuities as well. (Singh Y: 1973, 1987). The process reflects not a break from tradition towards modernity but modernization of tradition itself.

REFERENCES

Ames M.M. "Structural Dimensions of Family Life in the Steel City of Jamshedpur, India" in Singer Milton (ed.) *Entrepreneurship and Modernization of Occupational Cultures in South Asia,* Duke University Press, 1973.

Banaji J. "Chayanov, Kautsky, Lenin: Considerations Towards a Synthesis", *Economic and Political Weekly,* Vol. XI, No. 40, 1976.

Bhalla Sheila, "Agricultural Growth: Role of Institutional and Infrastructural Factors", *Economic and Political Weekly,* Vol. XII, Nos. 45, 46, 1977.

Cohen Allan, *Tradition, Change and Conflict in Indian Family Business,* Hague: Mounton, 1974.

Davis Kingsley, *Population of India and Pakistan,* New York: Free Press, 1958.

Desai I.P., *Some aspects of Family in Mahuva: A sociological study of jointness* in *a small town,* Bombay: Asia Publishing House, 1964.

Fox R.G., "Pariah Capitalism and Traditional Indian Merchants, Past and Present", in Singer M (ed) *Entrepreneurship and Modernization of Occupational Cultures* in *South Asia,* Duke University Press, 1973.

Goode W.J., *World Revolution and Family Patterns,* New York: Free Press, 1963.

Gore M.S., *Urbanization and Family Change,* Bombay: Popular Prakashan, 1968.

Gadgil D.R., *Origin of the Modern Indian Business Class: An Interim Report,* New York: Institute of Pacific Relations, 1959.

I.C.S.S.R., *Status of Women in India: A Synoposis of the Report of the National Committee,* New Delhi: Allied Publishers, 1975.

Kolenda P., *Regional differences* in *Family Structure in India,* Jaipur: Rawat Publications, 1987.

Krishnaji N., "Agrarian Structure and Family Formation: A Tentative Hypothesis", *Economic and Political Weekly,* March, 1980.

Mehta S.D., *The Indian Cotton Textile Industry: An Economic Analysis,* Bombay: 1953.

Mines M., "Tamil Muslim Merchants in India's Industrial Development" in Singer M (ed) *Entrepreneurship and Modernization of Occupational Cultures in South Asia,* Duke University Press, 1973.

Marriott M., "New Peasants in an Old Village", in Singer M (ed) *Entrepreneurship and Modernization of Occupational Cultures in South Asia,* Duke University Press, 1973.

Murdock C.P., *Social Structure,* New York: Free Press, 1949.

Moore W.E., *Impact of Industry,* New Delhi: Prentice Hall, 1965. Mukherjee R.K., *West Bengal Family Structures,* 1946-77, MacMillan, 1977.

Nandy A., "Need Achievement in a Calcutta Suburb", in Singer M (ed) *Entrepreneurship and Modernization of Occupational Cultures in South Asia,* Duke University Press, 1973.

Owens R., "Peasant Entrepreneurs in an Industrial City", in Singer M (ed) *Entrepreneurship and Modernization of Occupational Cultures in South Asia,* Duke University Press, 1973.

Patterson M.L.P., "Chitpavan Brahaman Family Histories: Sources for a Study of Social Structure and Social Change in Maharashtra" in Singer and Cohn (ed) *Structure and Change in Indian Society,* Chicago: Aldine Publishing Company, 1968.

Ross A.D., *Hindu Family in its Urban Settings,* Toronto: University of Toronto Press, 1961.

Saberwal S, *Mobile Men: Limits to Social Change in Urban Punjab,* 1976.

Singer M., "Indian Joint Family in Modem Industry", in Singer and Cohn (ed) *Structure and Change in Indian Society,* Chicago: Aldine Publishing Company, 1968.

Singer M., "*When a Great Tradition Modernizes: An Anthropological Approach to Indian Civilization,* New York: Praeger Publishers, 1972.

Shoji Ito., "A note on the Business Combines in India—with Special Reference to the Nattu Kottai Chettiers", *The Developing Economics,* Vol. IV, No.3, 1966.

Sujata K., "*Dynamics of the Family Firm in India: An Exploratory Analysis of the Role of Family and Kinship in Industrial Entrepreneurship*" M.Phil Dissertation, Jawaharlal Nehru University, New Delhi, 1982.

Spodek H., "The Manchesterisation of Ahmedabad", *Economic Weekly,* Vol. XVII, No. 1965.

Sivakumar S.S., "Family Size, Consumption Expenditure, Income and Land Holding in an Agrarian Economy: A Critique of some Populist Notions", *Economic and Political Weekly,* Vol. XI, No. 30, 1976.

Safa H.I., *Towards a Political Economy of Urbanization in Third World Countries,* Delhi: Oxford University Press, 1982.

Singh Yogendra, *Modernization of Indian Tradition,* New Delhi: Thompson Press, 1973.

Singh Yogendra, *Indian Sociology: Social Conditioning and Emerging Concerns,* New Delhi: Vistar-Sage Publications, 1987.

Timberg T.A., *The Marwaris: From Traders to Industrialists,* New Delhi: Vikas Publishing House, 1978.

Chapter 6

Law and Social Change

The interaction between law and society can be seen at several levels: the judicial process and its socio-cultural linkages; law as an indicator of the nature of societal complexity, and its attendant problems of integration; and finally, law as an agent of modernization and social change. A sociology of law would have to deal with all the above levels of interaction between law and society. In our analysis, however, we shall focus on the relationship between law and social change and modernization in the context of the Indian Society. Using a sociological perspective, we shall treat law in its institutional and historical contexts and analyze its dialectics with society in its broader social structural setting.

The Dialectic of Law and Society

The dialectic of law and society in India has been determined by historical experiences during the passage from colonialism to nationalism. In the course of this passage, the paradigms both of the social and legal systems have evolved. This process bears an acute imprint of historicity; yet, in the light of our observations of similar interactions between law and society in the industrially advanced western countries, some convergence of experiences at a universalistic level cannot be denied. The processes of law and social change in India, while in large measure unique, do share some commonalities with industrially advanced nations particularly the crisis and contradiction of the paradigms of law and society.

The primary components of legal systems and the paradigms of modernization of the industrially advanced countries are based on the ideology of rational utilitarianism. Their *Gesellschaft* mode of society implies movement from the status to contract; from community to individual, from participation to administration, from guild to state, and from empathy to selectivity. It was the product of the *laissez-faire* ethos of a market-oriented, non-personalized legal system. Bentham, Weber and Schumpeter, the mentors of this "rational legal order" created bridges between the legal system and the social structure. The crisis of the late 1960's early 1970's in the industrial societies gave impetus to the awakening of interest in the Frankfurt School of sociology, of neo-Marxism and phenomenological existentialism. These new interests tended to shift the pendulum, in ideological if not structural terms, towards the search for alternative models of both modernization and the legal system. This development is largely a product of the structural contradiction of the post-industrial society; it surpasses the ideological confines of the capitalist and socialist states. Kamenko and Tay have written:

> In the communist world, the tension is between revolutionary transformation and the desire for social stability, between mass campaigns and the provision of social and psychological security for individuals, social spheres and activities, between utopian spontaneity and technical-administrative realism. In the west, the crisis is a crisis in the individualistic view of society, in a legal model attuned to the need of the individual house or property holder, the entrepreneur, the settled citizen living on terms of equality with those around him, secure and confident as an individual in his bearing vis-a-vis the state and the rest of society. Against this, the new demands elevate the interests of "requirements" of the comparatively poor or underprivileged as contrasted with those who are "at

> home" with law: they pit the interest of "society"or of "humanity" against "excessive" respect for individual rights and powers, especially proprietarial rights and powers; they tend to see men as social products and not as free moral agents, as people to be cured or helped rather than judged. The new demands are suspicious of lawyers as a profession in the common law world because they see them as a privileged caste with guild traditions and powers; in Continental Europe they see them as characterless servants of state. (Eugene Kamenka and Alice Erh-Soon Tay, 1978:50-1)

This new perception of the legal system and its paradigm obviously inheres the contradictions of an industrial society: its increasing unidimensionality, its failure in the liberation of human personality, and its de-humanizing abstractness resulting in the alienation of man. This process represents a legal order which, in the course of the structural and normative changes that it brought about, also introduced seeds of disenchantment and mystification. This challenge necessarily brings sociological jurisprudence into full play as the social dialectic tends to deeply influence the legal system. It spurs the shift from

> Private law, concerned with the security of the individual, to public law, concerned with welfare and social utility. Even in the heart of the private law, in the law of tort or torts, and in contract, they have discerned similar developments. In torts there is the movement from the legal-individualistic principle of fault liability to the social, actuarial cost-benefit analysis that leads to the principle of loss distribution; in contract, the concept of a bargain struck between ideally equal and freely contracting parties is increasingly infringed upon by the courts' recognition of social and economic inequalities and of the one-sided restriction of the power to bargain by the

existence of standard contract." (Kamendo and Tay, 1978:48-9).

In addition to the above, new areas of law in the fields of industry, environment, consumer protection and social services have come into being. These fields are beyond the .nineteenth century conception of the common law and its judicial processes. The deeper implications of the changes in the industrial society are responsible for these legal innovations as the response to the demand for basic alterations of the paradigm of industrial society. Thus, the crisis of the legal system is also simultaneously a crisis of the industrial society. The transition from an industrial to a post-industrial stage of development ushers in social demands on the one hand, and structural changes in the society on the other. These structural changes especially in the society's modes of production and patterns of leisure time, necessitate redefinition of the legal order of society at the inter-personal, inter-group, and inter-societal or international levels. New meanings of "responsibility," "freedom," "civic culture," and "rationality" emerge. The structural changes which occur at the post-industrial stage of development tend to contribute to not only formal "differentiation" in roles and relationships, but also their "de-differentiation," "personalization," and possible revitalization of the principle of "status" in "contract." These changes may be made possible by the giant leaps in both technology and culture; they are already evident ill the current electronic and computer revolutions.

We have thus far discussed the challenges faced by the industrial societies at a higher stage of development. The dialectic of law and social change in the industrially developed nations has a historically endogenous character. The new challenges and contradictions that legal systems face in these societies are generally different from the ones faced by the developing societies. In the nations such as India, where a colonial interlude fundamentally transformed the indigenous evolution of the legal system, the early legal structures were characterized by the dualism of the indigenous hierarchical and colonial utilitarian traditions. The universalistic element in the contradictions, of the Indian legal system is confined to the utilitarian-Benthamite legal administration and philosophy which the British imposed on India. The British system is itself faced with contradictions in the light of the waning impact of utilitarian liberalism and the increasing demands of welfarism and socialism.

The dialectic of the' legal system in India, with its entrenched "multiplex of social structures" on the one hand, and its multiplicity of indigenous, colonial, and developmental traditions on the other, is tremendously complex. The significant element in the interaction between law and society in India rests on the heavy burden of these multiple traditions and the social concerns and orientations of each. The convergence between the dialectic of legal systems in the industrialized nations and the legal system in India points to the developmental phase of legal system in India following independence. The contradictions inherent in the administration of justice, exemplified by the conflict between abstract individual property rights, the pursuit of profit, and the protection of the weaker and more vulnerable groups, represents a crisis in the paradigms of both society in general and the legal system in particular in India. The situation in the West is similar, but probably less complex.

Law and Society in India

The relationship between law and society in India could generally be studied in three phases: the traditional or indigenous, the colonial, and the developmental. The indigenous legal system in India did not have a nomogeneous character. It reflected the basic features of the Indian social organisation; it was based on the principle of "inter-structural autonomy" (Singh Y:1973). The three basic components of the social system in India, the polity, the system of stratification, and the cultural norms, were relatively autonomous and unique. Under this sytem, the king or his administrative and judicial authorities constituted the top of the hierarchy; they were centers of redressal or appeal and they intervened in few cases. The custom prohibited the king from intervening in disputes related to -local customs, norms, and practices of castes, subcastes, or tribes. These groups had their own judicial processes through *panchayats,* community leadership of elders, or the intervention of the chief of the dominant local caste. The normative structures of the legal system were not totally integrated in the *Dharmashashtras,* the often quoted sources of the Hindu legal traditions. The system represented at best the principle of interpretation at times of dispute. Depending upon the exigency of circumstances, local priests and community leaders always had the right to new interpretation of the legal codes. And yet, there was a system in this judicial administration. The system was based upon the hierarchical order of authorities from the local caste, community and tribal *panchayat,* to the council of the dominant or ruling clans, to the court of the king. This linkage of judicial administration was also in consonance with the economic and cultural organization of the traditional society. The three territorial units-the village, the small town and the capital cities—were the focal points of social and cultural mobility on the one hand, and of nodes of commerce, administration, and political intercourse on the other.

In the studies of many scholars' who have commented upon the indigenous legal system in India (see Cohn, B.S.: 1961 and 1965, Gallanter, M.: 1972, 1968, and Kane, P.N.: 1950), one finds the focus on the diversity, and not the integrative principle, of the system. It may well be, as Bernard S. Cohn suggests, that in the eighteenth century, Indian social relations operated in a "multiplex" manner, "a relationship in which a person tends to occupy the same position relative to the same set of other persons in all networks of purposive ties-economic, political, procreative, religious, and educational." (Cohn: 1961:617). If, however, one considers the unit of interaction as caste or subcaste, the fluctuations of fortunes within each such unit of individual families would always cut across the matrix of multiplex relationships. This is the pehnomenon which still remains valid in India. The important feature in the indigenous legal system was, therefore, its sub-systemic autonomy. Despite the ups and downs in the polity in traditional India, the highly enduring and innovative sub-systemic autonomy persisted.

The main attributes of this legal system and its "judicial processes" were: large-scale participation, paternalism, flexibility, and innovative emphasis on compromise and hierarchy. Because community living in the *Biradari* or kinship group was the essential social matrix within which justice was sought, the resultant legal process was oriented more to "adjustment" than "judgement." This judicial process was as informal as it was in-expensive. It acted in harmony with the cultural ethos of hierarchy, continuity, and community ties. The role of dominant castes, families and kinship groups did occasionally vitiate the process of justice; this, however, occurred more frequently in the settlement of property and heredity disputes. Greater catholicity in the commitment to norms was observed in the larger towns where the *mahajana* supervised the justice of contractual obligations, trade and commerce.

The British who introduced the colonial legal system could never have a fuller appreciation of the traditional Indian legal system and its judicial process. It could not be understood in dissonance with the traditional Indian polity, economy and social structure. Their colonial interests were basically at variance with these institutions and their linkages. They overemphasized the elements of discontinuity and normative multiplicity because these elements worked well with the objectives of colonial appropriation and profit. The interests of both the British government and the East India Company coincided in these objectives. The need for "order", nevertheless led, to the imposition of a new legal system. The only legal system which the British administrators could consider viable was an improvisation of the Benthamite utilitarian tradition. There was, for a while, a debate between the modes presented by Cornwallis and Munro. Cornwallis opted for an embodiment of the commands of the government in formal legislative acts. He advocated administration by independent judicial administration in order to both secure private property and control the abuse of executive power. Munro, on the other hand, based his model on "paternalistic ideology" and assumed the role of personal authority to reign supreme in the Indian culture. Hence, his emphasis was on the evolution of a judicial system anchored in village *panchayats,* local customary tribunals of elders, and native judges. There was to be no complete separation between the judicial and executive functions. Though this debate continued for some time, and though Munro experimented with some elements of his system in Madras, the Cornwallis model of a legal system and judicial administration patterned after the British constitution and common law eventually triumphed (see Stokes, E.: 1959).

The judicial administration which Cornwallis imparted to India had come to stay. Its main features include: the establishment of a British-controlled court in every district to administer law and order, the administration of personal law in accordance with the customs of each religious group, and the settlement of revenue matters according to the principles of the pre-existing Muslim law of usage. In addition, judicial procedure was to be modelled after the British practice, judges of the district court were to be either British or British-covenanted civil servants (Indians could be recurited at lower levels), and the district courts were to be assisted in personal matters by Hindu and Muslim priests. A legal profession was to be established; land revenue was to be permanently fixed; individuals or corporate groups were to be recognized as owners of land for revenue payment; revenue and judicial functions of the administration were to be separated; and ownership were to. be settled in district, civil, and appeals courts (see Cohn, S.: 1961:614).

Codification accompanied this structure of legal administration. Macauley, president of the first Law Commission set up in 1834, produced the draft of the Indian Penal Code which became law in 1860. Between 1853 and 1870, the Law Commission contributed to the civil and criminal Codes of Procedure which were enacted in 1859 and 1861, respectively. At about the same time, India was given a uniform judicial structure as a result of the unification of the Supreme and Sadar courts into High Courts. The Law Commission's efforts also led to the enactment of the Succession Act (1856), the Limitations Act (1871), the Evidence Act (1882) and the Contract Act (1882). Under the direction of the government of India, there came a Specific Relief Act (1877), the Negotiable Instruments Act (1881), the Trust Act (1882), the Transfer of Property Act (1882), and the Easement Act (1882) (see Singh, Y.: 1973:98).

This spurt of legislation impelled the emergence of a radically different legal order and impinged directly and deeply upon the normative and cultural system of the Indian society. It was not only a measure of formalization, but also a mode of modernization through westernization.

The significance of the imposition of the colonial legal system in India was marked. It created a new class of professional legal experts, the lawyers, judges, court administrators, and bureaucrats. These are the basic components of a civic society. The introduction of the colonial legal system led to the arousal of aspirations and demands for positive rights by the deprived classes and communities. In course of time, it led to the growth of educated classes and to the creation of the substructure of a new middle class of capitalists, entrepreneurs, and civil servants. These and other sorts of professionals led the nation's movement towards independence. It is this movement which shaped the post-independence Indian Constitution and provided the legal boundaries for social change which exist today. The colonial process of modernization brought forth the sub-structural and sub-cultural character of social change which has remained an important feature of the Indian administration.

The inter-structural autonomy mentioned above enabled the new middle classes in the legal professions to emerge from the specific castes, communities and groups which already enjoyed a privileged position in the society. This made it possible to introduce social and cultural innovations without coming into conflict with the core of the structural and cultural foundations of the society—its caste structure and cultural ethos. The new forces of change thus could be absorbed and filtered through the middle classes to the rest of the society in gradual stages. The thirty-years of the nationalist movement in India served to forge these forces and aspirations for change into a national ideology. The contradictions now faced by the independent Indian state with regard to its legal framework for social change are anchored in the levels of incongruities between its social and cultural ideology and the structure of its legal profession. A social ideology which is based on secular, civic and egalitarian features naturally comes into conflict with a legal profession which is based on individual rights and class structure and is, at least in the abstract sense, unconcerned with collective responsibility.

Thus, the colonial legal system introduced new challenges and possibilities for social change in India. It did, however, also create legal institutions which were, in terms of pedagogy and procedure, alien to the general population's experience and reach. The new system did away with the traditional participant mode of justice which had operated via the courts of the *panchayats,* chiefs, and kings. It introduced systematic codification on laws which were rooted in the alien cultural and philosophical soil. These new codes replaced the traditional customs and conventions of the *dharmashastras, koran,* and *haidth.* It also rendered justice remote and expensive and clouded its functioning, in an atmosphere of mystification and suspicion. The result was the emergence of two cultures in the legal profession as it is organized in India today; these cultures are referred to by Marc Gallanter and B.S. Cohn as the "lawyer's law" and the "local law." The cultural hiatus that this dualism created in the realm of law and the legal profession is not specific to India alone, but is a general problem which occurs in the modernization of a traditional society which is characterized by a high level of historical and cultural depth. The crisis in cultural terms is a crisis of reconciliation between traditionalization and modernization.

Law and Society After Independence

The national movement in India which culminated in the independence of the country failed to create an indigenous legal system. Mahatma Gandhi did voice his suspicion of the British sponsored courts and the lawyers in his many exhortations of the civil disobedience movements, but when India gained her freedom and the framing of the Constitution began, the Gandhian emphasis on an indigenous legal system and judicial administration was not accepted by most members of the, Constituent Assembly. The Constitution as it emerged contained elements of the Gandhian ideology, including village *panchayats* and democratic decentralization, in the Directive Principles of the new state policy. As late as the establishment of the Ashok Mehta Committee on *panchayati raj* in the late

1970's, the Gandhian ideologues who advocated the complete decentralization and autonomy of the village *panchayat* system did not find full support. While evaluating the need for indigenization of the legal system, the Law Commission of 1958 did not see any major contradictions between the present legal system and the "genius" of the people (Government of India: Ministry of Law: 1958). It noted, that, "It is true that in the opinion of the Law Commission, the Indian legal system had, in the course of its functioning, undergone modifications adequate to render the imprint of the alien system more suitable to modern Indian conditions, Moreover, they agreed that, had the indigenous system been allowed to evolve independent of colonial intervention, it would have grown along a path similar to that of the present legal system. Such ideas lend perspective to the dilemma of the Indian middle class with regard to the challenges of modern nation building on the one hand and the rhetoric of indigenization on the other. Studies have shown that the dualism of the two traditions has been functionally well-adapted in the Indian legal system (see Khare. R.S.: 1972 and Gallanter, M: 1972).

One important innovation since independence is the introduction of the *panchayat raj* system in villages. Together with the community development activities, the *panchayat raj* also incorporates the system of *nyaya panchayats* for lower level judicial administration. Two national committees investigated the administrative and functional nature of these systems and decided to accord these *panchayats* the judicial power relevant to the day-to-day administration of justice. This decision was based primarily on the ideology of the village community, the role of participation, and the relatively informal judicial procedures which occurred without the intervention of lawyers. The introduction of these new systems rendered some levels of justice more freely available to the rural folk at a lower cost. They became more free from the legal substructure of the abstract rules and impersonal procedures. Subsequent evaluative studies carried out by state committees and research teams have, however, found that these *nyaya panchayats* are largely non-funtioning and are, for the most part, ridden with factious interests. Due to the system of elections which is used to select *panchas* or court members, the *nyaya panchayats* have become highly politicised. The states of Maharashtra and Rajasthan, whose committees reviewed the functioning of these village courts, have received recommendations for disbanding them. This coincides with the Law Commission's insistence that judicial and electoral processes be kept separate. Findings such as these again enmesh the state and the rural politics together and expose the structural contradictions and the alienation of the masses. As Upendra Baxi rightly suggests, this institution of otherwise great significance has not made an impact. He correctly attributes this to the ambiguity of ideology and the marginality of the institutional linkages which act as an additional constraint in their functioning (see Baxi, U.: 1982:323-7).

Law and Social Change in India

The ideology of social change which has been adopted by India after independence is enshrined in the Constitution. It incorporates the elements of both the liberal democratic values and the Gandhian values of social change. This can be discerned in the dualism found in the fundamental rights and the directive principles of the state policy. The former is rational, liberal and individualistic in ethos; the latter asserts the principles of communal welfare, decentralisation of power, amelioration of the condition of the weak, and commitment to the abolition of the "unhealthy" social practices recognised by the Gandhian tradition (i.e. liquor consumption, etc.). Whereas the Constitution recognised the individual as the unit for interaction in matters concerning legal rights, voting, state administration, it also recognised the legitimacy of specific castes and communities for special treatment. Examples of such groups include Scheduled Castes, Scheduled Tribes, religious minorities, and backward classes. The instrument of social change in this model is social legislation. Social justice, equality, secularism, and democracy are its fundamental normative goals.

The Constitution thus brings out two apparently conflicting principles: it presents universalism and particularism in the same ideological package of social change. Is this irrational? Is this a product of ad hocism or a quirk of history or the colonial legacy? Or, is this an eclectic effort to synthesize modern with traditional values in the ideology of change? Sociologically, the answer to these questions lies in the fundamental commitment that the nation has made through the Constitution to introduce changes in a peaceful manner (the Gandhian or later the Congress ideology) so that India could become a modern, secular, democratic and socialist state. Egalitarianism and freedom are difficult values to reconcile in the statecraft of a nascent democracy following its liberation from the colonial exploitation. Conditions arise which call for judicious and selective use of legislation for bringing about social changes commensurate with the objectives of the Constitution.

The civic model of change, as derived from the Constitution, could not logically recognize primordiality, caste, religion, and ethnicity. It could not leave the most exploited, the weak and vulnerable groups in the society at the mercy of the market forces of social change which always structurally favour the rich and the strong. Hence, reservations, protective discriminiation, and special favour to religious minorities and the weaker groups emerged. With the aid of legislative reforms, the strategy of change implicit in this model relies on the application of the pressure of social change through structural changes in the social, economic, and cultural systems. For this propose, the Constitution enjoins upon the executive, legislative, and judiciary special responsibilities; Justice Krishna lyre has very aptly analyzed this relationship:

> A collective consciousness which makes India great is that collective consciousness that makes every Indian feel elevated. Now, so I plead that the Constitution's code, its fighting creed, as has been put in the title of this talk, is not elitist. It is democratic. It is proletarian. It is people-oriented. Now, this people orientation must be manifest in the operation of the three instrumentalities which I called the Constitutional troika. The executive, when it operates, must function as if it has raised itself to the consciousness of the Constitution. In that event there would be no unimplemented laws which were enacted long ago. Likewise our legislature has to pass many laws. Mahatma Gandhi, in a publication "The Harijan" has-said, "I visualise Independent India to be again engaged only in making legislation after legislation to save the poor." There is so much to be done to save the poor. And all this must be by legislation because the executive has the authority only when the legislature passes a law. So, legislation must be made. Continuous stream of legislation, all welfare-oriented legislation. And then we come to the interpretation of these laws by the judiciary. No country can have a civilisation safe if it does not have a competent and independent judiciary. I emphasise competent judiciary as an important ingredient. An incompetent judiciary, a fraudulent judiciary, an absolutist judiciary, a judiciary given to judicial excesses, can be as dangerous as an executive given to excess. An absolutist executive, and absolutist judiciary and an absolutist parliament cannot be *persona grata* in a democracy. What we want is a judiciary which is accountable, a judiciary which is

> responsible, and with these parameters, a judiciary which is absolutely free, fearless and independent. If you seek to pressurise the Judiciary, then the poor will suffer. Because who has the ability to pressurise? It is the rich man who has got the ability to pressurise. (Krishna lyre, V.K: 1982:9-13).

The above interpretation of the intent of the Constitution is the most empathic. The Marxist interpretation, in comparison, treats the Constitution as a bourgeois document intended to perpetuate the capitalist state. The liberal interpretation claims that the Constitution is elitist and charges it with neglect of the egalitarian pursuits that pervade its corpus, from the Preamble through the Directive Principles. The question of interpretation apart, there is a logical principle and strategy behind the Constitution. One jurist has termed it "civic revolution." This differs from socialist revolution which is based on the open legitimacy of class struggle and its attendant socio-economic and political implications. India has deliberately chosen a path of development and social change which promotes social mobility, opportunity, and well-being of the deprived sections of society in a nation which is no doubt dominated by the rich and the elite. It does, however, employ a method of legal consensus which is based on a reconciliation model. In such a model, the responsibility of the dominant classes becomes acute because reconciliation implies, almost in a Gandhian style, the voluntary accommodation of the demands of the poor, the weak and the deprived, and the underprivileged. Its logical compulsion is more pragmatic than ethical; the privileged should know that such accommodation is also in their self-interest. In Marxist terminology, it is the tactics of the intelligent national bourgeiosie who, forewarned of revolutionary potential, attempts to contain it. One the contrary, the specificities of the Indian social structure and its historicity would show imperfections both logical and historical in the nature of alternative paths of development and modernization.

Indeed, the contradictions of the relationship between law and social change in India rest not so much in the inadequacy of the models as in the processes .of implementation and execution of these models as such. During the three and a half decades of functioning as a democratic nation with planned development, India has succeeded on many frontiers of social change. The landed aristocracy stands abolished as a class; the power structure in the villages has passed almost completely from the traditional rural elites to a new rural middle class. A new class structure has emerged in the villages and a peasant middle class, which is aggressively entrepreneurial, has quickly adopted scientific methods and techniques of agriculture and is the leader of the green revolution. The monopoly in higher education, previously a privilege of the upper caste and classes, has now slowly started percolating to the middle classes in the villages. These changes are a result of legislation and other reform measures. The reservations which the Constitution accorded in the legislatures, government services, and schools for the underprivileged have now successfully spawned a new generation of educated youth. New voices have been added to the demands for change and have contributed to the increasing mobilisation in the social structure.

The demonstration effect of these has been so acute that, in some pockets of the country, it has led to retroactive protests. In the field of land reform legislation, the ceiling level on land holdings which was enforced during the 1950's and 1960's has been further reduced in most Indian states. This is an indicator of the consciousness of reconciliation. The impact of land reforms, though uneven from state to state, has spurred agricultural growth and green revolution in several parts of India. This in turn has created a new phenomenon of labour migration from poorer states such as Bihar and Eastern Uttar Pradesh to states such as Haryana and Punjab. It has had far reaching social consequences in the liberation of the working classes in their home states from the clutches of the dominant classes or castes. It has provided new capital and savings for investment in land, houses, and cattle and it has opened up new possibilities for social mobilization and the independent political functioning of the working classes as a group. This has been especially true of the lower castes such as the Harijans and the Girijans. The recent increase in inter-caste tensions in rural areas is indeed a result of the trends of mobility in the rural social arena.

Another important area where "civic revolution" seems to have made a successful impact in India is in the area of electoral behaviour. Electoral awareness has increased throughout the country. as the election procedure has spread through the village *panchayats,* the *nyaya panchayats,* the assembly, and the parliamentary elections. Direct elections now dominate the selection process. In addition, there are electoral procedures for representation for several bodies of voluntary associations and cooperatives. The system of electoral politics and its concomitant consciousness have created a new sense of power and self-esteem in various segments of the rural and urban population. No doubt it has also activated factional politics and kindled a narrow breed of "casteism" and ethnicity. Sometimes, these identities emerge into communal principles in voting. If, however, we use voter participation as a measure, rural and urban participation in India is significant and comparable to voter participation in many developed democracies. This new electoral politics and participation rate has indirectly reinforced a vital component of the civic culture, the legal consciousness.

Another positive social change which has taken place following independence is in the field of industrialisation and growth of the entrepreneurial classes. The commanding height of economic power continues to vest in public sector industries. However, during the past three decades, a sizable middle class of small entrepreneurs, commercial classes, and professional groups has emerged in the urban centres. Together with the rural middle classes, these groups comprise roughly one-fifth of the population. The rise of this middle class is a stabilising and critical element in India's process of social change today. This class adds stability to the system, contributes to economic growth and mobility, offers employment opportunities, and makes use of public and private resources for development. On the other hand, this class suffers from the cultural gauchery of the new rich and is less scrupulous about conformity to legal norms and established middle class values. The middle class's demonstration effect on the social structure is both acute and deviant. Its approach to the weaker sections is more cynical and indifferent rather than cosmopolitan; it has, therefore, increasingly tended to flout the norms of "reconciliation" and "consensus." This is indicative of what is known as the "underdevelopment of development" process in India.

The positive direction of social changes has also taken place in the fields of science, technology and manpower. The population of scientific manpower in India is said to be the third largest in the world. Managerial skills and innovation, the credibility in science and scientific ways, has become deeply rooted in India, even down to the level of the remote villages. The traditional thought patterns have not, however; declined. There is a precarious and often dialectical coexistence of the two in the Indian society. The same holds for the nature of the legal profession. Related studies by sociologists demonstrate the persistence of a large body of traditional and non-rational practices both in the structure and the functioning of the legal professions and its organisation (see Gandhi, J.S.: 1982, Sharma, K.L.: 1982, and Oommen, T.K: 1983). The problem now confronting the legal system is the product of the process of "under development", of certain sections of our society in the wake of overall development and social change.

Contradictions of Social Change and the Legal System

The positive aspects of social change in India, as we have discussed above, have generated a substantial number of contradictions in the social system. The rise of the middle class in villages and cities has led to hostile attitudes toward the weaker sections .and the poor. In villages, the tensions between the Harijans and the- Hindu upper castes have increased and necessitated the passage of the Civil Rights and Disabilities Act. The act makes derogatory reference to the Scheduled Caste status as a cognizable offence. The exploitation of the labourers by rich peasants held under bondage through the extension of loans has been held legally void, but there is evidence of its perpetuation. Minimum wages for labourers in the unorganised agriculture sector stands as one piece of evidence of failure and the lack of uniformity in the introduction of small scale enterprises and shops is another. Similarly, effective legal norms with respect to the vulnerable sections of society—the children, the prisoners, the women, the prostitutes, the slum and pavement dwellers–do not exist; or, their existence is rendered feeble by the resourceful, powerful, and influential vested interests in society.

The development aspects of social change in India have given birth to a new awakening among the SC, the ST, the poor, and the working classes. Evaluation studies show that social and economic reform measures undertaken by the state for the benefit of these groups are not successfully reaching them. In areas where these groups are sizable or organised, these changes often culminate in protest movements. Although these movements are effective for the redressal of grievances, but they are isolated and scattered events. Unfortunately, the intervention of social workers is inadequate and rare.

In the wake of increasing social awareness of the asymmetry of the development process–the gaps between the rich and the poor, the agricultural labourers and the rich peasants, the basic contradiction facing the Indian legal system is met in the efforts to make the instruments of legal protection, legal bargaining, and legal redressal available to all. Greater emphasis has been given to this field over the course of the past decade. A movement for "legal aid" for the poor and destitute has begun. A government appointed committee has made a report on the implications and modalities of the legal aid movement. There has, in addition, been a significant response from the bar and from the bench. The Supreme Court has recently allowed third party petitions by voluntary social workers and associations on matters of social concern. It has instituted investigations into several matters on the basis of legal aid and legal rights to all citizens. Until a few years ago, this would not have been possible.

Nandita Haksar writes:

> Now a public spirited citizen, concerned lawyer, or journalist, or a democratic rights organisation can move the court on behalf of an oppressed or exploited person or group of persons. The court will recognise their locus standi (legal standing). This right was first recognised in the famous transfer of judges case and later elaborated in the Asiad case. This was in conformity with the trend in other parts of the world. (*Hindustan Times,* New Delhi, May 22, 1983)

Supreme Court judgements are binding for all courts of the land; therefore, the initiative of the court with regard to its decision to allow third parties to be represented in matters of social justice and social concern has tended to set in motion a new democratisation process in India. It is reported that hundreds of requests for legal aid are now pouring into the courts. These letters are addressed directly to the judges of the Supreme Court. The cases of the bonded workers in Haryana, of the prisoners (undertrials) in Bihar, of the inmates of the women's rescue home in Delhi, of the children in juvenile institutions, and of the torture of ordinary citizens by the Army in Nagaland, just to name a few, demonstrate the wide spectrum of the new movement for legal aid. A new area of what is called "public interest litigation" has come into being. It is being run by public spirited jurists, social workers, journalists and politicians. Several organisations which are working for the protection of the democratic rights in India have been established. Considering the vastness of the country and magnitude of the population in need of such legal protection, this new development has touched only the fringe of the problem. The movement has, however, by selectively addressing the most critical issues of legal aid, already made a very significant impact.

The impediments of this movement toward social change may be observed in the indifference, or even hostility, of the executive and the political functionaries. There are many feudal impediments in the Indian political and civil service systems which make it necessary that some aspect of the legal aid movement be institutionalised by the government. As we have mentioned, the democratic development in India is bound to create an upsurge among the rural and urban poor, and their protest movements are bound to grow (see Desai, A.R.: 1983). The "civic revolution" as a model of social transformation would make it a logical necessity that law as an instrument of social change is held under constant review. More importantly, the judicial processes and legal administration, and the role of the executive in the proper implementation of the legal norms, should be rendered more effective. Finally, the efforts of the Indian government and the efforts of the public organisations and enterprises working to advance the movement of democratic law and social change must be linked.

REFERENCE

Baxi Upenra: *The Crises of the Indian Legal System,* New Delhi: Vikas Publishing House, 1982.

Cohn B.S., "From Indian Status to British Contract", *Journal of Economic History,* 21-613-618, 1961.

"Anthropological Notes on Disputes and Law in India", *American Anthropologist,* Vol. 67, No.6, 1965.

Desai A.R, *Sociology of the Underprivileged,* Inaugural address, 5th U.P. Sociology Conference, Kanpur, University of Kanpur, 1983.

Gallanter M, "The Aborted Restoration of Indigenous Law in India", *Comparative Studies in Society and History,* Vol, 14, No. 1, 1972.

"The Displacement of Traditional Law in Modern India", *Journal of Social Issues,* Vol. 24, No.4, 1968.

Gandhi J.S., *Lawyers and Touts: A Study of the Sociology of the Legal Profession,* New Delhi: Hindustan Publishing Corporation, 1982.

Haksar Nandita, "Justice For the Common Man", *The Hindustan Times,* New Delhi: May 22, 1983.

Iyre V.K. Krishna, "The Indian Constitution: Our Founding Deed and Our Fighting Creed—Some Thoughts on Their Future", First S.K. Sinha Memorial Lecture, New Delhi: 1982.

Kamenka D, and R. Tay Alic Erh-Soon, "Socialism, Anarchism and Law", *Law and Society; The Crisis in Legal Ideals,* ed. Robert Brown et, al., London: Edward Arnold, 1978.

Khare R.S. "Indigetfous Culture and lawyers law in India", *Comparative Study in Society and History,* Vol. 14, No.1, 1972.

Kane P.V., *Hindu Customs and Modern Law,* Bombay: Bombay University, 1950.

Stokes Eric, *The English Utilitarians and India,* Oxford University Press, 1959.

Oommen T.K., "The Legal Profession in India: Some Sociological Perspectives", *Indian Bar Review,* Vol. X, No.1, 1983.

Singh Y, *Modernization of the Indian Tradition,* New Delhi: Thompson Press, 1973, also, "Legal System, Legitimation and Social Change", *Aspect of Changing India,* ed. S.D. Pillai, Bombay: Popular Prakashan, 1976, pp. 381-4.

Chapter 7

Structure, Tradition and Indian Societal Resilience

The term societal resilience is to be understood in its contextual sense to be meaningful as a framework for analysis of social processes in the developing societies. The context lies in the. past history of colonial exploitation and neo-colonial threats to these societies, and the continual attempts by imperial nations to dominate their economic, political and cultural autonomy. The fragility of the institutional foci in these nations gives a poignant meaning to the notion of resilience. The, resilience of societal structure and tradition connotes the ability of the developing nations to withstand socially, culturally and economically the forces of instability both internal and external to their system as they plan their march towards modernization. Obviously, the term societal resilience is to be understood not in a literal sense; such as statusquoism or static consesuality in the system. It is to be used as the contextually relevant notion or even a process through which the crises of cultural, economic and political identity of the 'new' nations in Asia, Africa and Latin America are articulated leading to the evolution of a meaningful strategy for their autonomous process of development and modernization.

The historicity of social transformation in each society in this context assumes great significance. The process of modernization needs to be analysed in the background of history and tradition of each society to fathom the potential of its societal resilience. This is important because it is observed that the initial impact of the forces of modernization generates social, and cultural tensions in most societies which put to test their capacity for societal resilience. Otherwise, it leads to cultural and institutional breadkdown in societies resulting into their dependency upon 'big powers' leading to neocolonial relationship of subordination. Consequently the democratic processes are subverted, cultural institutions are debased and a psychology of disenchantment from one's own tradition comes into existence and becomes a source of ever widening cultural alienation. The nations that get caught into this relationship of neo-colonialism have certain institutional and social historicities which need to be analysed to grasp the significance of societal resilience for successful modernization.

Social Structure and Resilience

Social structure and its historical specificities influence the degree of resilience that a social system has in withstanding the challenges of development and modernization. In the Indian experience, such historical forces were defined by inter-structural autonomy within the society. The impact of initial forces of technological, institutional and cultural modernization coming through colonialism was encapsulated by the social system because of the autonomy among its major structural foci, such as the polity, social stratification and value system. The inter-structural autonomy in the Indian society has subsisted through its tradition and past history. As a result, the exogenous impacts, political, economic and cultural, were moderated or even encapsulated in the system through selective adaptation which helped their indigenisation instead of their creating forces of disenchantment from the native tradition. The traditional Indian society was characterised by substantial autonomy between the roles of the literati or priest who served as spokesman for dominant values and cultural practices and the political rulers (or kings) who held power. In a symbolic form, this is exemplified in the Indian tradition by the autonomy or even superiority of the 'priest' over the 'king' in matters concerning tradition or its interpretation. This autonomy added to the resilience of the Indian society and its tradition. Even if the political institutions came under stress or were over-run the cultural tradition maintained its autonomy of form and functions. Just as the priests did not enjoy legitimacy for influencing the functions of the political institutions (except in rare instances), the rulers too were subjected to compliance to the priests in matters of normative-pronouncement on values and tradition.

Similarly, the traditional institution of social stratification, which was characterised in India by the varna-caste hierarchy, functioned almost autonomously through the caste panchayats, jajmani networks and its self-governing guilds. The caste panchayats dealt with most matters related to the economic, social and cultural practices, customary rights and duties and in rare or exceptional cases did the members of a caste approach the court of the king or the state for settlement of disputes. This gave caste system not only a regional character but also cultural, economic and social autonomy from both the interference of the political rulers as well as the Brahmin priests. Indeed, the relationship between the priest and the castes in traditional India was of curious sociological significance. Priests did not enjoy a uniform access to roles in ritual practices of each caste as such. Their relationship with the lower castes and outcastes was always marked by segregation; they did not enjoy uniform respectability from a large number of middle-peasant castes. Only in relation to the upper castes did the priestly calling have a relationship of sustained ritual interaction. Even here, the priests were accorded superior status only in matters relating to the ritual practices. In the realm of power and social hierarchy a rich member of the upper caste, say from the ruling clans would not accord the priest a superior status. In such matters, ritual obesiance to the priest did not accord with higher social status of the priest.

These structural features of the traditional Indian society rendered it possible for the society to assimilate new external values and institutions selectively without being swept over by the impact of their cultural, political and economic forces. It enabled the social system to maintain a remarkable degree of continuity with change. This process was put to severe test following the establishment of the British colonial rule in India. The contact with the western cultural tradition through colonial rule was for India in the nature of an encounter of a historical kind. It represented an encounter of a technologically and scientifically stronger tradition inhering modernization values of rationality, enterprise and industrialism with one which was suffering from its inner tensions and institutional disarray. Such an encounter, in a colonial setting could have swept India from its cultural roots but for the resilience of its social system resulting from the historicity of its social structure and tradition. The impact of westernization in the initial stages of the colonial rule was moderated in India through a process of structural encapsulation. This is evident from the fact that the educational, economic and cultural policies that the British introduced in India during the 19th century only succeeded in creating a middle class largely confined to the metropolitan cities, big towns and upper castes.

The social background of this middle class, which emerged as a result of the colonial form of modernization had features which initiated the freedom movement on the one hand, and on the other, encapsulated the impact of the western cultural onslaught and tensions of the colonial penetration. Thus, the social and cultural forces such as values of equality, legal rationality, technology and science which this western contact generated were structurally confined to a limited group and the system gained time for slow percolation of these values to the rest of the society through an adaptive process of transformation. It did not cause major dissociation in the established institutions, values, social structure and tradition. Eventually, the growth of national independence movement which in the beginning was elite sponsored, gained a mass character under Gandhiji's leadership. It made it possible for an alternate ideology for India's social, economic and political modernization to evolve with wider sensitization of people to this ideology. The historical forces in the society imparted a social resilience to the system that it could after independence undertake a massive and revolutionary programme of political, social and economic modernization despite the human cost of partition. The partition was the result of the colonial design to subvert Indian forces of nationalism and battle against imperialism. The colonial policy of divide and rule for a moment proved stronger than traditional forces of resilience in the system and the country was partitioned on *communal principle* of two-nation theory which Indian leadership refused to recognise and even today does not accept.

The second phase of modernization began with the achievement of Independence at the end of the colonial rule. Long before this, the Indian national movement had contributed to the growth of modernization and development ideology for the Indian society. As the national leadership took over the reign of the government this ideology was given a paradigmatic shape through the Constitution.

The paradigm of modernization derived many elements from the Western tradition, such as the emphasis on rationality, secularism, parliamentary form of democracy, adult franchise and a rational judicial and administrative system, etc.

The Constitution, however, also incorporated many elements from the Indian .nationalist movement and history, such as emphasis on social justice, moral bases of the directive principles of the state policy, the provision for protective discrimination for scheduled castes and tribes and special provisions for the religious minorities, backward classes and women. It also laid emphasis on maintaining the positive aspects of the Indian culture and tradition in the process of economic development and modernization. *Thus, the paradigm of modernization which India adopted after Independence was itself a measure of resilience of its social structure and values.* At the same time it set into motion forces of transformation in society which increasingly put the burden of proof about societal resilience on the historicity of its processes and their social framework.

Tradition. Structure and Resilience

The first issue that emerged soon after India embarked on the path of parliamentary democracy with adult suffrage was as to whether its people, illiterate and traditional as they were, would be able to absorb the tensions released in the process of electoral participation. Could parliamentary democracy succeed in a society where most people were unlettered? While posing these questions, it was overlooked how a people with centuries old heritage of civilization also intuitively imbibe skills through enculturation and non-formal education that serve as instruments both of succourance and catalysis in discerning political participation. The erroneous assumption was to equate 'illiteracy' with lack of 'education'. The 'education' to which in a broader sense the people were already exposed to through mass participation in the national movement was overlooked because the analytical model was imitatively borrowed from the West. The electoral politics and the level of political participation in India on the contrary has shown remarkable resilience through its responsive character and feed-backs from interest groups on issues of devolution of powers, social policies and finer electoral discriminations in respect of voting for Parliament and the Assemblies. Even though the structure of party system in the country has not yet stabilised, a framework is already emerging of coalitional strategies between the regional and national political parties which is in consonance with the Indian social and cultural pluralism and its historicity. The process is yet in the making.

Yet another negative prognosis on the role of tradition and traditional values in the modernization of Indian society was based on the argument of the other-worldly orientation of Hindu values which were expected to retard successful industrialisation and economic growth. This too has been proved to be wrong as the evidence from the pattern and direction of entrepreneurial activities. and people's active participation in industrial work in all parts of the country suggests. In the villages, even the puritan Brahmins have not hesitated from sericulture (which meant killing of silkworms, a practice not approved by tradition) when they realised its economic advantages. The industrial work force, even those producing traditionally polluting commodities such as the leather goods and chemicals, has turned out to be fully representative of the social spectrum comprising all castes and creeds. *This falsifies the assumption that caste and religion would hinder the process of industrial modernization.* Studies of urban centres in various parts of the country have established that religious gatherings such as the 'Hari Kathas' and prayer assemblies not only preach religion but also serve as means of communication of messages relevant to modernization ideology of the country, such as social reforms, upliftment of the status of women, curbing the practice of caste discrimination and other social evils. Such media have also been made use of by contending political groups and parties, even the parties professing radical left ideology.

Such uses of the traditional institutions and values in the promotion of modern institutions and values have established a successful strategy of modernization with the continuity of tradition.

This is further evident when we observe the role that traditional joint family structure has been playing in country's economic and industrial modernization. Even during the British period when the business houses in India were not encouraged to establish industrial units in competition with the British concerns, and when credit was not available from the government sources, the joint family and kinship resources of the members of the business community were successfully utilised for raising capital for investment in industrial units in the country. This has been specially true for the cotton textile mills in Maharashtra and Gujarat during the early twentieth century. The same pattern has also continued after Independence despite governmental support for capital funding as an organic element of the planning process. The studies of industrial entrepreneurships, their life-cycles, rise and fall as conducted by social anthropologists have revealed that *there exists a causal relationship between successful functioning and growth of an industrial unit and the internal cohesiveness among the members of the family* which owns and manages the enterprises. There are instances of disintegration of industrial entrepreneur;. I units following partition in the joint family of the entrepreneur house-holds. It is also found that 'managing agency' system of ownership of industries or firms in India has its basis in the family structure.

A more prominent relationship between the joint family structure and economic development in India has been highlighted in the studies of the agricultural development called the 'green revolution'. It has ensured not only food self-sufficiency but also food surpluses to the country. Studies of social structure and values system of the farmers involved in green revolution bring out interesting sociological features which establish the case for continuity of tradition in the process of economic modernization. The leaders of green revolution in all parts of the country come from the traditional peasant castes, normally the middle castes which have had centuries old tradition of cultivation on land as their calling. The mode of their work on the farm holdings invariably is oriented to the joint-family partnership. This not only ensures efficiency but also economy in the process of production. *The joint family mode of production nevertheless also selectively includes elements of rational uses of technology,* such as uses of new variety of seeds, fertilisers, pesticides and rational methods of irrigation essential for higher yield. It also makes use of modern techniques of marketing, banking and credit along with utilising the resources of traditional family and kinship ties. This is combined with continuity of such traditional values of peasant castes as frugal style of living, consumption mainly of the traditional items of food, clothing and living, etc. and careful family budgeting. These contribute to higher economic surpluses which are used not only for further economic modernization and expansion, but also for incurring expenses on such traditional items as marriage feasts, construction of houses, temples and sacred ponds, etc. in villages. All this suggests a curious amalgam of tradition with modernity in the modernising economic and social profile of the countryside in India today.

These sociological facts amply reveal the continuity of tradition in the process of modernization of economy, social structure and value system of the Indian society. Such adaptive tendencies have been consistently observed in the emerging functions of institutions of religion, caste, family and kinship and folk cultural tradition. It is a measure of the resilience of the traditional institutions in India that most of them have been successful in effecting a selective and rational adaptation to modernity, without creating major social hiatus in its social structure or tradition, This process has prevailed in India throughout the 1950's to 1970's. This period can be identified as carrier of the second phase of the modernization process in India.

As we mentioned earlier, the first phase of modernization coincided with British colonialism when this process was largely confined to the urban middle classes and existed in an encapsulated form. The period after Independence enlarged the social base of modernization and set into motion social, economic and political forces which had far reaching consequences for all segments of the society. The policy of protective discrimination for the scheduled castes and tribes together with adult franchise in their electoral participation energised them for new scale of social participation and social mobilisation. It also generated social conflict which could largely be accommodated in the social system not only through progressive incorporation of these groups in the political processes of the society but also through implementing the policies of distributive' justice. Soon after Independence *caste-vote-banks played significant role in influencing the political and electoral behaviour of parties and people in India.* It led to politicalisation of castes, emergence of caste associations and backward caste and class movements. A surface view on these developments might make them appear like articulation of traditional institutions or their re-invigoration. A deeper evaluation of their structure and functions, however, reveals a much different story. These developments represent not the traditionalisation of the forces of modernity in society, but modernization of its tradition.

The second phase of modernization can be marked for its focus on capital investment for industrialisation, growth of technology, science, education, agriculture, energy and economic infra-structures, etc. on the one hand, and on the other, major social and economic reforms. The abolition of zamindari, agrestic serfdom, tenurial reforms, ceiling on land holdings, etc. explicate nation's commitment to establishing an equalitarian society. The nation-state with its ideological commitment to secularism, democracy, social justice and pluralistic values reinforced its legitimacy through these reforms. The new investments both in terms of capital resources and innovative institutions accelerated the process of social mobility and also generated social conflicts. Both were inevitable, because society was passing from traditional state of its static equilibrium to the state of dynamic equilibrium through social and economic modernization. Consequently, the pressure of interest groups, caste associations and backward classes increased for social mobility and economic development as a large segment of the deprived groups desired such opportunities traditionally. As a result of these processes the social system as a whole witnessed some major changes such as the abolition of landed aristoracy, emergence of middle caste and middle class dominance in urban and rural parts of society because of the opportunities made available to them through development planning initiated by the state, growth of new enterpreneurial classes in cities in sectors of small scale industries, trade and market enterprises and noticeable upward social mobility from among the deprived castes and classes as a result of protective discrimination in their favour. Even though its incidence was often localised, was uneven or differentiated compared to mobility among other social groups and classed, in qualitative terms it marked a major social change. The extent to which these castes and classes witness improvement in their social and economic condition remains a matter of debate among social scientists.

Consensus, Conflict and Societal Resilience

The resilience in the social and cultural systems of the developing societies depends upon their balanced growth within and regulation of forces from without that influence their process of social transformation. Among the external forces the neo-colonial designs of 'big' nations assume a great deal of significance. An effective strategy of social and economic growth necessitates that nations in the developing world evolve a paradigm of modernization which is commensurate with their culture, history and specificities of social structure. They may also have to work out a strategy of their relationship with 'big'-power nations, specially with a view to safeguarding their cultural and political freedom. Such paradigm is necessary because modernization inevitably activates social tensions, generates social inequalities and crisis of aspirations in the initial stages, in large segments of society.

Although the normative principles of modernization for India have been enunciated in the Constitution, the paradigm of modernization that India has adopted is reflected in its planning and development strategy. It comprises a *consensual approach to development and modernization, is based on principles of pluralism, decentralization and distributive justice* to be achieved through a rational legal path of democratic participation. It combines with state control over high points of economy with capitalistic mode of industrial and agrarian development. It calls for a strategy of development in which dissent and protest as democratic means of interest articulation are recognised as legitimate. These processes also help in the modernization of society through dynamic and pluralistic consensus building among contending interest groups. It extends not only to the relationships among the classes, caste groups, or communities but also to the regions, states and, centre and political parties in the regions. The consensual paradigm of modernization adopted by India implies that social conflicts resulting from economic development require continual review of policies and management strategies of social change. The focus should continuously remain on twin strategies: first, growth and secondly, with growth distributive justice. The emphasis on protective discrimination for deprived sections of the people provided in the Constitution accords fully with this paradigm of modernization.

A consensual paradigm of modernization is indeed organic to the democratic process of development. The threats that most developing nations which adopt this paradigm encounter are both ideological and social structural. These threats are interrelated. The social structural forces give rise to counter-consensus ideologies and reinforce the forces of regression and conflict. Most developing countries witness a rise in the size of middle classes as economic development gathers momentum. Since Independence there has been a substantial growth in the middle class population in the social structure in India both in the countryside and cities. *The green revolution in agriculture contributed to the rise of middle class, middle caste peasantry.* In cities, a large segment of the entrepreneurial, professional and administrative personnel belong to the middle class. Most people in the services, education, journalism, media and public utilities jobs also give rise to the middle class-caste population. *The growth in the middle class structure has accentuated the crisis of aspiration among the rural and urban poor, the scheduled castes and the tribes.* The condition of the poor has no doubt improved as a result of economic growth and modernization. But the relative rate of improvement in the condition of the poor sections of society has remained comparatively slower. Hence a rise in their aspirations and social consciousness generates conflicts and social disaffection. The result is more tension, inter-caste feud and communal violence.

The consensus ideology of modernization, in operation since Independence, was designed to overcome such conflicts through social reforms, economic growth and distributive justice, The abolition of Zamindari, and ceiling on land holdings came soon after Independence. Later, the nationalisation of banks followed in order to release more resources for programmes of poverty removal and social welfare for the poor. By the 1970's most states also introduced protective discrimination in favour of the backward classes to improve their share in higher education, administrative jobs and in government sponsored programmes of economic growth and modernization. These policies effectively helped in conflict resolution and consensus building in most parts of the country, but such a process is an ongoing one and calls for changing strategy both qualitatively and quantitatively as the process of modernization proceeds. The consensus paradigm succeeded not only in social and economic domain of modernization in India but also in stabilising the centre-state relationship, particularly in overcoming separatist movement of the fifties in the southern Indian states. The reorganisation of state boundaries on linguistic lines was a similar consensual strategy for political accommodation of regional, cultural and economic aspirations within the framework of a nation-state.

Communalism, Conflict and Social Resilience

When we evaluate the efficacy of the consensus paradigm of modernization for building resilience in the social system in the wake of forces of social transformation, we find that it has proved more effective in. the management of social structural tensions than ideological ones. Consensus strategy has to a large extent contained the conflicts based on caste and class in the countryside and cities. It has been helpful in the management of inter-state, inter-political-party and centre-state relationships. It has maintained its legitimacy through policies and programmes of removal of poverty, of social welfare and protective discrimination. In the ideological realm, however, consensus ideology in India has always remained on trial, as in this domain it had to reckon with communalism ideology promoted by the colonial rulers which resulted into the partition of India. The British colonial policy was systematically oriented to encouraging the ideology of communalism in India, be it of inter-caste, inter-tribal, caste-tribal or inter-religious nature. The consensus paradigm of modernization which India adopted after Independence offered also a strategy for containing the communal challenges. The Indian leadership at no stage accepted the colonial communal ideology, the communal awards or the view that religious groups constitute separate nationalities in India. The 'two nation' theory based on religion was repugnant to national leadership as it was designed to weaken the forces of nationalism and the emergence of Indian nation-state.

Conscious of the threat that communal ideology posed to the balanced process of modernization in India, the religious minorities have been provided many Constitutional safeguards to protect and promote their cultural and religious identities. At the political level, the communal (religious) ideology of nation-state suffered a big set-back when Bangladesh broke away from Pakistan disproving the religious theory of nation-state. This established the validity of the secular ideology propounded during the Indian freedom movement as a basis for cultural and political modernization. Nevertheless, the dimensions of communalism in India have assumed a multifaceted character, such as casteism, tribalism, regionalism and religious fundamentalism. These communal forces have since Independence posed a continual ideological challenge to the paradigm of modernization and the process of social and economic growth in India. During the early two to three decades after India gained freedom, the communal ideology derived its strength mainly from the exploitation of the economic, social and political deprivations of the minorities and deprived castes, tribes or religious groups. Communalism was used as a source for mystification of largely non-communal grievances. To use a technical language, it represented a false consciousness, This variety of communalism could easily be taken care of through the consensus paradigm of modernization of which the emphasis on growth with social justice was an organic component. Since the 1970's onwards communalism specially of the religious variety has taken a new form, that of religious fundamentalism. Unlike the former pattern, it does not necessarily arise out of poverty or social or economic deprivation. Rather, it tends to grow with higher levels of economic development achieved by emergent new classes or groups within the minority religious communities. Its focus is not merely on improving the economic, political and social life conditions of the religious group as such but on converting them to a counter modernization ideology. It exhorts minorities for going back in time and postulates a religious worldview as a total alternative to the secular scientific worldview of a modern society. It postulates an overarching role for religion not only as an ethical system which governs personal faith, rituals and ways of life but also the economic, legal, political and social institutions. Religious fundamentalism does not believe in separation of politics from religion, which is a challenge to the secular rational bases of cultural and political modernization. It is not only regressive but also obscurantist in character.

The Indian social and political institutions have shown enough resilience despite many ups and downs in containing communalism of the false consciousness variety. Its modernization paradigm has a built-in strategy to overcome strains generated by communalism. Partly it can be resolved through rapid economic growth and effective enforcement of the policies of distributive justice. The surveys on the changing economic and social conditions of the Muslims in various parts of the country reveal that all those among them who come from artisan occupational category have adjusted well to new entrepreneurial activities and have not only improved economic and social status but have also generated employment potential for others. The institutional agencies such as the Minority Commission and Voluntary groups engaged in the economic and social welfare of the religious minorities, particularly the Muslims are steps towards containing the communal forces of the fundamentalist variety. These, however, pose a challenge to the resilience of the Indian social and political institutions as quite often such forces may be sponsored from outside the country. Communalism was used as a weapon by the imperial and colonial forces it; the past, and there is no reason to believe that such forces might not be active again to retard the progress of autonomous growth of the Indian nation-state. *Its back-wash effect on the system, particularly the communalism of the majority community, the Hindus, may pose, in this context, a far more dangerous challenge than the communalism or fundamentalism of the minority communities.* That Hinduism as a religion encourages values of tolerance, pluralism of faith and rituals or that it is a religion without a Church might harmonise with the secular ideology of modernization but the potential for its communalization in the contemporary historical context exists and it should be fought with all our determination. It calls for adequate institutional and political responses from our political parties and intellectuals.

As the process of economic development gathers momentum, the level of people's awareness of social, economic, political and ideological issues becomes sharp. This should by itself help reinforce institutional foci which have been created by the nation to overcome the forces of communalism and fundamentalism. However, additional institutional mechanisms may have to be devised. There is also a need for more effective monitoring and implementation of the programmes of distributive justice and .civic rights, specially of the minorities and weaker sections of society. The roles of mass media, education and voluntary agencies in institutionalisation of the Indian paradigm of modernization can be termed as crucial. So far, despite continual challenges from communal forces, from within the country and without, India could adhere to its modernization paradigm based on secularism, socialism and democracy. This has been possible because of the innate flexibility of this paradigm and also due to the strength of the Indian civilization. The contemporary challenges, such as the rise of fundamentalism in Punjab and communal conflicts in other parts of the country can be seen largely as products of social frustrations generated by the contradictions of economic and social growth. For instance in Punjab the rise in communal violence is found to be related to the alienative tendencies among peasant youth due to lack of employment opportunities commensurate with their rising aspirations. With higher levels of agricultural prosperity achieved by the Punjab farmers, aspirations of their younger generation have risen higher. Agriculture no longer offers them satisfaction in terms of employment opportunities, especially of the kind aspired for. The lack of rapid industrialisation reinforces this alienation further reinforcing the potential for violence. Most other forms of communal movements also owe their origin and legitimation to similar social and cultural conditions, although the combination of specific factors might vary. *Adequate institutional responses together with more economic growth and industrialisation can help us meet the challenges of communalism and fundamentalism in India.*

Contemporary Restructuration and Societal Resilience

The cumulative result of the processes of modernization in India since Independence have set into motion a massive process of social restructuration. Through this India enters into a new phase of modernization. Its societal resilience is also put to new strains. The economic growth so far achieved has generated opportunities, enhanced social mobility, brought into dominant position a new middle class both in the cities arid villages. The scale of professionalisation in the services, utility agencies, etc. has reached new high points. The successive electoral participation by the people, their exposure to mass media and the political, social and cultural movements have hightened their level of consciousness and non-formal education. This has increased the cultural and motivational displacements among various classes, castes and communities. A great deal of structural inter-meshing has resulted among these groups based on the asymmetry of the principles of wealth, power and level of education. The community structure in India, be it of a caste, religious group, tribe or territorial group, no longer remains homogenous. The process of social mobility through new jobs, education, enterprises, access to political offices, etc. have severly fractured the homogeneity of communities, and made it possible now to look at the Indian structure in terms of categories, such as occupation, class, ideology, etc. rather than as communities such as caste, kinship, tribe or religious groups. The process of restructuration is increasingly eroding the community base of the social structure and slowly bringing into being alternate principles such as of class and category as elements of organisation of society.

The process is a natural result of investment in modernization. But it also generates contradictions of serious proportion in the process of transition. No structural transition has ever been painless in history, but the democratic process of the Indian social transformation has been based on the premise that human cost of this transition must be minimised. The resilience of the system and its paradigm of modernization can be tested in accordance with its success or failure in achieving this objective. How far is India able to achieve this goal? What are the sociological symptoms in this regard? Answer to these questions assumes significance for the Indian situation today, faced, as it is with gigantic phenomena of restructuration in society. The direction in which society is moving is indicated by the impact that modernization forces are having in the creation' of alternative social structure by fracturing the traditional ones which were based on caste by classes, professional groups and social movements in urban areas. Massive migration of the rural population to cities goes on alongwith this process. Many social reform movements are going on in India today which are organised not on the principle of caste, religion or community but on secular principles, such as the commonality of interests, skill and knowledge and commitment to social responsibilities. The social movements in the field of women's status, about ethicization of professions, the legal aid movements and the voluntary groups for the development of the deprived sections belong to a new category altogether. The organising principle of such movements is not primordiality such as caste, kinship or community, but one's status as a citizen of the Indian republic. Many social movements in some parts of country aim at generating humanistic awareness among people about science and technology and its role in society. The people's movement about generating awareness of environmental problems created by unplanned industrialisation and its dysfunctions have also been increasing fast during the decade of the 1980's.

These developments augur well for realising the Indian goal of modernization. Its impact, however, still remains limited in size and spread though strong in qualitative terms. The principles of caste, community and religion continue to articulate themselves as interest groups in the system. The significant change is the historical disjuncture today between the principles of community versus category in the processes of social restructuration in society which differs from the pattern of the 1960's and 1970's. In the decade of the 1980's the traditional institutions instead of wholly succeeding in adapting the modern institutions and values within their framework are slowly giving way to institutional replacements and differentiation. This process indicates a qualitative shift in the pattern of social transformation in the Indian society. Despite the fact that it generates tensions or even occasional violence, it is a measure of assertion of the element of resilience in the Indian social system to cope up with processes of modernization. In the new social formations, traditional institutions instead of absorbing the functions of the modern sector are most likely to undergo differentiation of forms without, however, fully eroding the traditional institutions and value orientations.

Chapter 8

Ethnicity, Unity and Indian Civilization

The process of nation-building and economic development in India has thrown up social forces which can perhaps be appreciated better in the context of its history and civilization. It is not easy to comprehend the nature of the Indian civilization in its totality given its great historical depth, multiple social and cultural overlaps and a great variety of little traditions which its 'great tradition' encompasses. Even as great traditions, Indian does not have one but many great traditions, although the Hinduistic tradition has always enjoyed a position of overwhelming significance. Islam, Christianity, Budhism, Jainism, Sikhism and several tribal traditions have existed and enriched the civilization of India, which is an ensemble of these great and little traditions of cultures and ways of life. Overarching these many traditions in the Indian civilization is the influence of the western tradition of social, economic, cultural, legal and political institutions which historically has superimposed itself on the indigenous civilization. K.M. Panikkar has aptly described it saying:

"The inheritance that India has stepped into is only partly Hindu and Indian. The inheritance from the West is not less important in many fields. Modern India does not live under the laws of Manu. Its mental background and equipment, though largely influenced by the persistence of Indian tradition have been moulded into their present shape by over a hundred years of Western education extending practically to every field of mental activity. Its social ideals are not what Hindu society had for long cherished, but those assimilated from the West and derived predominantly from the doctrines of French Revolution, and to a lesser, though to an increasing, extent from the teachings of Marx and the lessons of the Soviet experiment. Even the religious beliefs of Hinduism have been transformed substantially during the course of last 100 years. In fact, it will be no exaggeration to say that the New Indian state represents traditions, ideals and principles which are the results of an effective but imperfect synthesis between the East and West". (1963: 15-16)

For the Indian civilization, the encounter with the West was a major challenge as the principles which this civilization represented diverged greatly from the traditional principles of Indian civilization. We have described the traditional principles of the Hinduistic civilization of India which dominated over other cultural traditions for centuries as those of *hierarchy, holism, continuity* and transcendence. Of these elements hierarchy was shared in the worldview of several non-Hindu cultural traditions as well. So was the principle of holism. In other words, emphasis on communal bonds and religious-customary segregation of social strata was a feature of most communities and cultural groups in India with possible exception of the tribal communities in some pans of India. The Western civilization which encountered the Indian tradition was not only colonial and expansionist politically but culturally it represented a very strong counter force to the Indian tradition. It was a product of the French Revolution and Industrial Revolution. Its principles of *equality, civic-individuality, historicity* and *utilitarian rationality* were at least in theory in acute contradistinction with the normative principles of the traditional Indian civilization (Yogendra Singh: 1973). The process of change that this encounter with the Western civilization set into motion in India has resulted largely in adaptative transformations. This possibility has been due to the centuries old process of cultural assimilation going on in India that gave its civilization a measure of internal resilience. Talking about this. feature of the Indian civilization Lord Mestion wrote:

> "There has been nothing, or very little of clash between her own ancient culture and the alien culture imported from the West, no violent conflict of ideas or methods, no forcible replacement of one social system by another. The more fitting metaphor would be that of a stream of new thought and practice flowing into the sea of Indian traditions and life. We can trace, for a time at least, the distinctive colour of the river, spreading out over the surface of the sea; but, as we often have cause to reflect in India, how little can we tell of its influence in the ocean depth beneath" (Introduction to P.J.O. Malley's *Moslem India and the West* (OUP) quoted in Panikkar: 1963:17)

Diversity, Unity and Indian Civilization

This brings us to the problem of diversity in Indian traditions and cultures and its bearing upon the process of unity of the civilization. This unity could be observed at several levels, especially in the periods before the Western encounter. An important source of unity can be noticed in the processes of cultural and technological communication and interaction. N.K. Bose identified the role of travelling mendicants, traders, story tellers, craftsmen and artists in traditional India who established cultural bridges of unity between regions and cultural traditions. The institutions of pilgrimage, fairs and festivals provided yet another nodal points for communication for cultural unity in the framework of its diversity. Bose writes: "Although, India was, by and large, illiterate, yet there was built up certain mechanisms by means of which common intellectual and emotional elements of culture were brought to the door of the most distant communities, isolated either by geography or the promotion of social separatism" (1977:6). In addition to these agencies the social structure and economy forged linkages of reciprocity and interaction between regions, groups and cultural traditions. This is exemplified in the studies of elite-folk cultural and administrative continuum in India. The organisation of Indian cultural tradition at the levels of the folk and the elite have had a large measure of mutual give and take through localisation of the cosmopolitan or elite traditions and cosmopolatization of the local traditions. This also extended to the levels of social and cultural mobility in the system.

Although never fully exhaustive, the political economy of the imperial system in traditional India did create administrative, educational, technological and cultural institutions and personnel whose role was cosmopolitan rather than local. These institutions functioned as bridges among local social systems and cultural traditions. This was also reflected in the inter-structural autonomy of traditional Indian social structure under which the cosmopolitan institutions of polity, culture norms and systems of social stratification provided a measure of variety, freedom and creativity for local institutions. Indeed, the traditional caste panchayats and panchayats of the occupational groups specially the artisans, craftsmen and service communities such as the washermen, barbers and potters, etc. who were linked together under the jajmani system, enjoyed autonomy in both self-governance and for enforcement of rules of reciprocity with the larger society. The role of the cosmopolitan political and administrative institutions in their functioning was only as appelates in extraordinary situations. There was a continual circulation and mobility from the local level of technical and artistic personnel to the cosmopolitan levels, a process in which the mobility from the village, to small town, to capital city was a natural corollary of the achievers in various fields.

The unity through this diversity of cultural and social

forms in traditional India was articulated in commonalities of social and cultural institutions, occupation and technology, trade, market and transport, etc. which brought a measure of functional interdependence among the diverse cultural group identities. This was also balanced by a relatively static level of population size, easy availability of land resources through reclamation, or through other means and the slow pace of technological innovation in the realms .of culture and economy. These features, on the one hand promoted isolation and preservation of cultural and social identities and on the other, allowed communication process that established linkages towards unity both formal and substantive.

Ethnicity and Indian Civilization

There is a sharp debate among Indian social scientists whether the notion of 'ethnicity' is appropriate in analysing the processes of cultural and social identity formation in Indian society. Even in general sociology, the term ethnic was 'used to indicate belonging to a nation, especially a pagan one', according to *A New Dictionary of Sociology* (G.D. Mitchell 1981). The term denotes a group with its own customary ways and culture, but it is broader in connotation than the concept of nationality as it "permits non literate peoples to be identified as social aggregates in the same way as more advanced peoples and nations. The Germans, the Jews, the Gypsies are all ethnic groups, also are Congo pygmies and Trobrianders" (Mitchell:1981:69). Yet another *Dictionary of Sociology* (Abercornbie, Hill and Turner:1984) is critical of the term 'ethnic group' for the confusion in its connotation With genetic or racial constitution as the basis of solidarity. Such a view is rejected by sociology as it does not accept that notion of human groups can unambigously be derived in terms of their genetic constitution. It prefers to formulate this concept rather in processual terms as formation of consciousness of identity in terms of culture, custom, way of life and language, etc. that emerges through encounters with other groups asserting domination or control. It says: "There is difference between a group which claims ethnic distinctiveness and one which has distinctiveness imposed upon it by some politically superior group in a context of political struggle. Ethinicity may, therefore, become the basis either for national separation or, for political subordination. The ambiguity of the definition of 'ethnic group' thus reflects the political struggle in society around exclusive and inclusive group membership" (Abercombie et al:1984:83).

There are many studies of the tribal, linguistic, religious and cultural groups in h1dia which either directly or indirectly use the notions of ethnicity to analyse its social processes. With few exceptions, most such studies show sensitivity to treat ethnic-identity in a dynamic setting, such as resulting from the process of migration of population from one region to another (see, Weiner Mynon:1978), cultural and political articulation (see, Oommen T.K:1985), the movements, etc. (see, Dipankar Gupta:1982; K.S. Singh:1977 M.S.A. Rao:1978 Yogendra Singh:1987). Most these studies rather than using ethnicity as a central notion for analysis have dealt with linkages that social, political, cultural and economic changes in society have with the emergence of separate identities, tribal, territorial, religious and political etc. These new group identities do not always conform with the notion of ethnicity as used by social or cultural anthropologists, particularly in the North America from where this concept got into wider circulation.

To our mind, the use of the term 'ethnicity' or 'ethnic group', to describe the social reality of the pluralistic Indian civilization, is out of place for various reasons. Firstly, because the analytical power of the notion of ethnicity lies not in, its facticity as such but in its operation as a process. Ethnicity as a process of cultural, linguistic and social-political self-consciouness of groups has little sociological significance as an isolated phenomenon. Such self-consciousness or sense of identity is, a universal phenomenon in all cultural groups. What converts this social self-consciousness into an ethno-consciousness contributing to social, cultural, political and economic demands in the process of social and economic change in society is sponsored by the state or results from the free market forces of economic and social development. The significance of ethno-consciousness lies, therefore, in the frame of reference of the 'other' group, community, locality or organisation which is perceived as unsympathetic, hostile or exploitative in relation to the indigenous group. The sociological phenomenon described as ethnicity is, therefore, a process rather than a substantive sociological category.

This is exemplified by the fact that ethnic conflicts and ethnic self-consciousness result invariably from perceived or real experiences of domination or subordination of one group by another either politically, economically, culturally or socially. A caste group, tribe, linguistic, religious or cultural group might, therefore, assume the functional equivalent of an ethnic group in its competitive quest for access to resources without empirically, however, qualifying as an ethnic group *per se*. This is so in societies with a wider historical canopy of civilization under which plural, cultural and social practices, "customs and values subsist and flourish. The context of a 'civilization society', therefore, alters the meaning of ethnicity altogether if it does not nullify its substantive significance. The students of ethnic processes in India have not been able to examine this aspect of its sociological significance because their analysis is devoid of a civilizational frame of reference in the treatment of supposedly-ethnic processes in the Indian society.

A distinction can, however, be made between two types of studies of ethnic processes within the Indian society:

first, studies which examine religious and cultural traditions and their appeal for forces of nativism, localism and communalism. Such studies can hardly ignore the context of civilization. Secondly, the studies of ethnic processes which do not derive ideological inspiration from any world religion, such as Hinduism, Islam, Christianity or Budhism, but rationalise their demand in terms of purely native traditions and conditions of social, political and economic deprivation. The communal territorial movements such as the Shiva Sena in Maharashtra belong to the first category. The movement in Assam also has had, despite variations, similarities with the former. The movement of the Gurkhas in West Bengal, the Sikhs in Pub jab, and the tribal groups in Nagaland, Meghalaya and Bihar fall in the second category. The study of the Shiva Sena movement in Bombay has revealed that 'practical ideology' of this movement (nativism) is couched within the 'worldview' of Hinduism of sort which is professed by its leaders (Dipankar Gupta:1982). Similar instances have been reported from Islamic fundamentalist movements, where the threat to the faith or its decline constitutes a general matrix for articulation of the specific social, cultural, economic and political demands. The reference to religion, particularly the 'world religion' (with basis in civilization) is made consciously in order to derive advantages in mobilization process and generation of resources to sustain the movement. The other type of ethnic mobilization which is based purely on native or local (little) traditions draws support for its ideology mainly from the existential and emotional conditions of deprivation of the people. Even though being a part of a 'world religion' such as Hinduism, the Gurkhas hardly seek rationalisation of their movement through religious affiliation. What matters in their case is the strength of their communal mobilization based on identity consciousness as a deprived and neglected group.

A distinction may be drawn between civilization oriented

nativistic movements in India and those that are anchored entirely in the local or little traditions. The concept of ethnic movement can possibly be applied more justifiably in the latter cases rather than in the former. It would appear that the notion of ethnic movement in the context of Indian social structure and civilization may need to be qualified with reference to the level of interaction and articulation of identities. Ethnic group implies homogeneity of culture and social structure on the dimensions of territory, language, culture and custom. Such groups are limited in number in India. We find that Indian social scene is easily identified through conceptual categories like caste, tribe, community, class, language, religion and region. Political mobilization of caste groups on horizontal lines led to emergence of the 'caste associations' on a large scale which have been studied in depth. Some tribal movements which are oriented to demands for autonomy in political, cultural and economic fields may qualify as ethnic movements because of the localization and structural-cultural homogeneity of their population. Otherwise, it is well known how the same tribe may be internally differentiated on the grounds of religion (converted and non-converted), dialects, access to wealth and power or even customary practices and life styles. Hence, ethnicity in the Indian context could at best refer to processes of mobilization of social categories and communities for self-conscious articulation of their social, cultural, economic and political developments in society. This could be held valid only in specific situations of structural and cultural homogeneity of the groups concerned. In other contexts the processes of mobilization takes place on the basis of caste, language, territory, religion or political-economic issues.

The social categories like caste, language, religion and region, etc. have a pan-ethnic character. The linguistic re-organisation of states in India after Independence was based on similar erroneous assumption that a linguistic community articulated homogeneous social group phenomena. Forty years after Independence we find that a variety of new interest-groups have emerged within linguistically re-organised states on the basis of caste, religion and territory. The Indian social structure and civilization cannot be understood on the basis of a single principle of social organisation, be it caste, religion, language or community. Each of these manifest vital elements of the Indian social structure and its civilization, but none of them individually encompass its totality. An organic pluralism is inherent in the principles which define the Indian civilization and its social structure. Empirically, caste is a local phenomenon, only its ideology (varna) has an extended, may be all-India meaning. But over a period of time, caste both structurally and ideologically has penetrated several other religious and cultural traditions, such as Islam, Christianity and Sikhism, etc. A· religious definition of caste ideology, such as through Hinduism, would not explain its role and significance in the Indian society. Similarly, religion arid language, though indicative of groups solidarity at a certain level are fractured by differentiation of such groups on the basis of caste, region, occupation and wealth. Within each religious, linguistic, tribal or caste group there are factors which articulate their internal similarity, but there are also strong elements which outcross each respective bond and unite with those based on dissimilar principles. There is diversity, but it also has a framework of unity.

Framework of a Civilization

The role of ethnicity, territoriality, religion, etc. in the integration of Indian society can be appreciated in the framework of its civilization. A common mistake in formulating the notion of Indian civilization is in identifying it predominantly or entirely in terms of the dominant

Hindu tradition. Indeed, the concept of civilization as it has evolved in sociological vocabulary precludes the use, of religious-cultural traditions to define it. In the western social science, the term civilization is associated with the rise of social, economic and intellectual institutions coinciding with the breakdown in the bases of feudal social organisation and the rise of ideas and institutions resulting in the evolution of a civic society. It also connotes social progress through growth in economy, technology and science, political institutions and culture. All these social elements are defined in secular-rational rather than theological terms (See, G.D. Mitchell: 1981:27). The notion of civilization docs have a cultural connotation but its significance lies in the growth of values and norms conducive to the development of a civic-industrial society away from authoritarianism of the feudal-theological systems. The notion of civilization comes closer to the concept of modernization popular ill contemporary sociology.

In the Indian context too, civilization as a social process transcends religious traditions, even though its structure and form may bear imprint of several such traditions, Hinduism, Islam, Christianity, etc. in various measures. Basic to the meaning of civilization are the techno-economic values, Institutions and social organisations that emerge in response to the forces of social, political and cultural development in society. Culturally, the emergence of urban centres, formalisation of aesthetic and intellectual creativity, predominance of the written over the oral informal mode of expression, and the emergence of specialised cultural and intellectual functionaries and institutions, etc. mark the transition from the pre-civilization to civilizational stage of cultural transformation. The role of intellectuals and cultural specialists with full time professional vocation inaugerates a departure from the folk mode of the pre-civilization stage of culture. Civilization depends for its growths on a certain level of economic and political development through which specialised functions and institutions of culture, learning, administration, polity, trade and commerce, etc. evolve and are institutionalised in society. It differs from precivilization stage of society intrinsically in terms of quality, but more important, it strengthens linkages between structures and institutions reinforcing societal unity. It forges regional social formations into a broader unified system of social, political and economic organisations culminating in the formation of nation-state.

Indian civilization has evolved through many stages providing a network of institutions and ideologies which offer unity in plurality. These institutions and their normative principles do reflect the cultural-religious traditions of Hinduism but these also transcend its confine and emerge as a composite system of values, norms and styles drawn from various cultural traditions. This is what constitutes the integral structure of the Indian civilization. It includes systems of political organisation, of control and administration of revenue, trade and market, military bureaucratic systems, the intellectual accomplishments in medicine, science, art, architecture, music, drama and dance forms, etc. which represent a synthesis of many forms and styles, and combine the sacred with secular in its structure and function. A closer study of these forms and their normative framework reveals creative orchestration of elements from several cultures and civilizations. Civilization provided functional linkages to myriad cultural and structural traditions and entities in Indian society through a pluralistic mould of sharing arid inter-dependence along with autonomy and segmentation. Inter-structural autonomy existed in the framework of unity of civilization (see, Singh Y:1973).

The process of Western contact through colonialism introduced a qualitatively new orientation. The British followed a mutually contradictory policy in pursuit of their colonial objectives: first, their policies activated the regional, religious and segmentary impulses of people in India. The British administrators-cum-social scientists usually constructed Indian society on a religious model derived from the dominant Hindu traditions. It overlooked the institutions of linkages between segmentary structures, such as caste, tribe, village and territory which the Indian civilization provided in the past. On the contrary, it emphasised the autonomy of each segment to the exclusion of inter-dependence. This set into motion fissiparious tendencies in society and enlarged the territorial, religious-communal consciousness among people which separated communities and groups rather than linked them together. The British due to exploitative character of their rule had to introduce technological, industrial and economic-administrative measures which had a macroscopic extensions, such as the railways, factories, workshops, roads and highways, police, army, judiciary and bureaucracy, etc. Slowly, in course of freedom movement the British also introduced political reforms which laid the foundation of civic culture and democracy. Paradoxically, the British policy on the one hand, strengthened the forces of regionalism, casteism and communalism and on the other established institutions for a pan-Indian consolidation of colonial state with imperial dimensions.

This contradiction of the British policy has cost the country a great deal in course of its political freedom and also in social reconstruction of society after Independence. It created a social situation in the country in which a dualism between principles of primordiality such as territory, religion, language, caste and tribe, etc. and the principle of civic rights like universal suffrage, democratic freedom of participation and equality, rational-secular judicial administration and education, etc. had to be recognised. The Constitution of India, which was framed after Independence, reflects and incorporates this dualism. It propounds the foundations of a civic society based on secularism, rationalism, freedom and equality. At the same time it also recognises the special rights and privileges of those sections of Indian society which were exploited for centuries or which feel insecure due to their minority status in, the society. The reorganisation of states soon after Independence on linguistic lines also reflects the sensitivity of Indian leaders to reconcile the aspirations of regional and segmentary entities with that of the aspiration to build a modern secular, democratic, socialist nation-state.

Diversity, Reconciliation and Unity

Ethinicity in the form of an encapsulated consciousness of culture, customs and ways of life becomes more articulate through encounter with, civilization which represents processes of modernization, economic, political, technological and scientific. By itself, ethnicity as a sociological phenomenon is retro-active in nature. Most issues which lead to the rise of ethnic mobilization seek recognition of their distinctive status and represent demands in social, cultural, economic and political fields. These demands take on meaningful shape only when the pace of modernization acquires a certain pitch and penetrates encapsulated structures of ethnicity and primordiality. As such, these demands can also be seen in a normal process of uneven pattern of growth towards modernization.

A large part of these demand related ethnic movements can be resolved following a strategy. of *constructive reconciliation.* The policies of the Indian state have been responsive to such demands in large measure and have yielded good results in the past. The examples are the separatist movement in Tamilnadu during the 1950's, and the recent Assam and Mizo accords. The strategy of reconciliation through accords goes together with the processes of planning, economic growth and policies of distributive justice in society. It is the process of upward social mobility and rise of a middle class among the ethnic groups and minorities which gives fillip to demands of territorial, parochial and separatist nature. The policy of reconciliation should, therefore, help in abolition of the deprivations of such groups both at the existential and cultural levels. The constitution of India is in a way designed to promote reconciliation policy in a constructive fashion. It also sets a limit to this process. The means must remain non-violent, and democratic and goals must not transgress sovereignty of the state.

The pursuits of the goals of social justice and social reconciliation in today's demand politics in the Indian society has assumed complexity because of ethnic-non-ethnic divisions. Where ethnicity is clearly demarcated, such as in the tribal groups, a uniform reconciliation strategy through social, economic and political measures could be undertaken. But in case of the non-ethnic groups, such as caste, religious communities and territorial groups we find no homogeneous social base for clear pursuit of such policy. The Akali separatist movement in Punjab is a glaring example. It sets its goals beyond the limits of the Constitution. Reconciliation with such demands poses organic threat to the very edifice of the Indian nation-state. Short of the demand for a theocratic political set-up, many channels for reconciliation of other demands of the Akali movement could be accommodated through democratic processes.

The other examples are the territorial movements for Jharkhand and Gorkhaland in eastern India. The former has a very long history whereas the latter is of a relatively recent origin. These movements demand separate state within the Union for their self-governance: The irony is that most such demands continue to emerge from states which were earlier reorganised on linguistic lines. As the processes of development; particularly growth of education, politicalization, aspiration for social mobility and social justice gain momentum, it is presumable that more and more sub-regionalisation and sub-ethnification of identities would take place. Hence, a reconciliation strategy anchored in creation of smaller and smaller states may not succeed in accommodating or defusing such demands. It may even prove to be counter productive. Yet, given our political framework of democratic participation and decision-making the principle of reconciliation cannot be forsaken.

Reconciliation Strategy

The reconciliation strategy embodied in the Constitution offers two types of policies for nation-building in India. First is the positive discrimination in favour of the traditionally deprived and exploited sections of society. Secondly, a broad rational policy of social, economic and political development based on principles of civic culture and judicial, administrative and institutional modernization where not the group but individual is recognised as the unit of operation. This dualism has been historically necessitated. It has also served the process of growth of Indian nation-state well. But in the process of growth new adjustments within the dual policy, which we characterise as the policy of reconciliation is necessary. The first element of this policy requires its systematic rationalisation. It may involve in the first instance its depoliticalisation to the extent possible. We notice that most demands by sections and groups are based on issues which have a political-economic character and can be met within the framework of the constitution. But, this can be a success only if reinforced by suitable social and economic policies. These policies would have to be evolved in an inter-related fashion as they are organically inter-linked. Some of the policy measures may be outlined as follows:

(1) The cultural and social institutions of the minorities, ethnic groups and communities must be jealously protected, and wherever possible opportunities may be

given for their constructive reinforcement so that cultural, emotional and social deprivations may not lead to frustration and alienation.

(2) This policy may be backed with measures of economic development of the groups with suitable mix of the policies of macro and micro planning supported by voluntary institutional efforts. The focus should increasingly be on decentralisation and self-help, so that specific nature of the economic deprivations could be looked after and removed.

(3) The policies with regard to education, information and communication may be suitably formulated to take into consideration two factors: first, the need to create man power and skill among the deprived groups, tribes and communities rendering their social mobility possible; secondly, providing a basis for their participation in the macro-social institutions of culture and development in the country. The media policy should also orientate itself to the need for a balance between the projection of the local, regional and national levels of social, cultural, economic and political profiles of people. In educational institutions too much regionalization due to linguistic demarcation of states has led to negative outcome such as decline of standards and loss of national perspective. It may be necessary to introduce a mix of both regional and national perspectives by amendments in admission, curriculum and employment policies. This could be done in stages through democratic avenues.

(4) There is need for consciously developing linkages between the regional and national institutions of planning, development and social reforms taking into view two major elements: participation and interdependence. The regional or local level groups, sections and communities be given a sense of participation in the national level institutions and must be made

conscious of their reciprocal responsibilities. So far, most local and regional interest-groups look at the national institutions only from the perspective of demand without having a corresponding awareness of their own obligations. This must be redressed through suitable administrative, social and political initiative. It is true that processes of industrialization and modernisation do strengthen macro-linkages in the nation-state, but these are also sometimes perceived as threat to local institutions and aspirations. Disinformation plays a role in such processes and a conscious initiative is, therefore, necessary.

(5) Finally, it may be recognised that a modern nation-state must have an efficient and strong support from reinforcement agencies of state policy such as the police, paramilitary forces and the army. Writing about the evolution of the French nation-state Theodore Zeldin aptly makes the point that French nation had to be *created* out of provincial consciousness in which middle classes, politicians and the army played a major role (Zeldin Theodore: 1979, 1980).

All these strategies must, however, be subordinated to the totality of the national ideology of political, economic and social development governed by secular, democratic, socialist and non-violent principles. India's strength in nation-building lies in its legacy of the non-violent tradition raised to the level of a political craft by Gandhiji. This set the foundation of the strategy for reconciliation. It could well be sustained.

REFERENCES

Bose N.K., 1977 *Culture and Society in India,* New Delhi: India Publishing House.

Gupta Dipankar, 1982 *Nativism: in a Metropolis: Shiv Sena in Bombay,* New Delhi: Manohar.

Abercrombie N, Hill S and Turner B.S.: 1984, *The Penguin Dictionary of Sociology,* New York: Penguin Press.

Mitchell G.D., 1981. *A New Dictionary of Sociology,* London: Routledge & Kegan Paul.

Oommen T.K;, 1985 "Insiders and Outsiders in India: Primordial Collectivism and Cultural Pluralism in Nation-Building", *International Sociology,* Vol. 1(1), March.

Panikkar KM., 1963 *The Foundations of New India,* London: George Alen and Unwin.

Rao M.S.A., 1978, *Social Movements in India,* Vol. I, New Delhi: Manohar.

Rudolph L.1. and Rudolph S.H., *In Pursuit of Laakshmi,* Hyderabad: Orient Longman, 1987.

Singh Yogendra, 1973 *Modemisation of India Tradition,* New Delhi: Thompson Press.

_____1987, *Indian Sociology: Social Conditioning and Emerging Concerns,* New Delhi: Sage-Vistar Publications.

Singh K.S., 1977 "From Ethnicity to Regionalism: A Study in Tribal Politics and Movements in Chotanagpur from 1900 to 1975" in S.C. Malik: *Dissent, Protest and Reform in Indian Civilization,* Simla: IIAS.

Weiner Myron, 1978 *Sons of the Soil,* Delhi: Oxford University Press.

Zeldin Theodore, 1979 *France* 1848-1945: *Politics and Anger,* New York: Oxford University Press.

_____1980 France 18(8-1945: *Intellect and Pride,* New York: Oxford University Press.

Chapter 9

Social Processes and Dimensions of Indian Nationalism

A sociological perspective has two distinctive advantages: first, it views nationalism as a social process and not as a formal structural construct. It treats nationalism with a degree of methodological elasticity and portrays it at various levels of its functioning in a dynamic interactional setting. Secondly, sociologist's attempt is always to examine a social process in terms both of its intrinsic character and also as an element in the general forces of social transformation in society. Instead of taking an isolationist view, sociology attempts to offer 'explanation' wherever it can, in a broad historical and culturally specific setting. It offers a blending of micro-history with macro-history and of theory with practice in society. No doubt, such effort has its hazards, specially of stepping into terrains unknown. It might also lead to oversimplification of issues that are far too complex. Yet, a sociological treatment of nationalism in India may be useful for two basic reasons: first, its conceptual formulation involves issues which are common to Indian social sciences viz the Western origin of its categories and their relevance. We have had a long debate in sociology on this question and shared experiences may have some validity. Secondly, sociologists in India have been engaged in intensive observation and analysis of diverse social processes in society, particularly those related to values and social structure, which might offer new insights into the problems related to social framework of Indian nationalism.

We come across several distinctive conceptual formulations of Indian nationalism both by our own and foreign scholars. A dominant view, that of historians and sociologists, sees the rise of nationalism in the context of British colonialism and the distortions it created in social structure and ideology of our society. These distortions refer to class character of nationalist leadership and its social, cultural and economic policies. It is said, these colonial distortions contributed to the rise of communalism, partition of the country and persistence of communal politics even after independence. Yet, it is recognised that colonial contact though subversive, generated social and economic forces that gave rise to nationalism and national movement in our society. In this approach, the study of relationship between social structure and cultural ideology forms a relatively weaker link. Its historiography draws heavily from policy framework and pronouncements of nationalist leadership and other agents involved in the Indian national movement in order to construct a social morphology of nationalism. It focuses upon macro-historical processes, their intricate movements, their filter-down effects and patterns in society. The basic tension between nationalism and communalism, its linkages with class structure, the role class structure plays in the power structure, and the evolution of secularism as an ideology after independence are analysed at a general level. It does not, however, examine these issues, as a sociologist or social anthropologist does, in the context of micro-historical processes and their given normative framework in the I social structures, such as caste, community, family, kinship, locality, region and belief system, etc. The indigenous cultural traditions are not examined closely in formulating social contexts of communalism and secularism and their implications to Indian nationalism. It is not able, therefore, to establish fully the linkages between the top and the subterranean levels of mobilization of nationalist consciousness and its structural tensions. Without fuller understanding of such linkages a sociology of Indian nationalism remains inadequate.

We have come across contributions of some historians and social scientists who show sensitivity to the problems of linkages. They find macro-historical analysis of nationalism and national movement in India to be dominated hy elitism either of liberal or marxist variety. Such historiography of Indian nationalism suffers according to them, by colonialist-elitism or bourgeois nationalist elitism, an 'ideological product' of the British rule in India. They suggest an alternative model for understanding national movement and nationalism which derives its inspiration from structuralist theory. The model proceeds through constructing a series of binary opposites such as elite versus subaltern, vertical versus horizontal mobilization, formal (cautious) versus spontaneous sources of movement and to delineate national movement as a dialectical process. The national movement and the ideology of nationalism according to this view suffered in India from structural cleavages between the 'mass mobilization' on horizontal lines and its vertical mobilization by elite nationalist leadership. The mass movement was located in principles of kinship, caste, class and territory, it was spontaneous in making and aimed at social resistance against exploitation. Its mobilization was not based on formal ideological or legalistic strategy, and it could change course and operation in midstream. The national movement led by elite leadership made use of such subaltern mobilizations selectively. The subalternity could not forge national movement all by itself. Yet the elite leadership, it is held, did not help forge these movements into a united front for social mobilization, due to its own class ideology. It created a structural hiatus in nationalist mobilization for large scale social transformation. This hiatus and the failure of our nationalist leadership according to this view, constitutes the problematique of Indian nationalism even today.

This viewpoint recognises the role of linkages between the pan-Indian and local mobilizations in the formation of political consciousness but its characterization of these linkages through notions of 'brokerage' or 'collaboration' neglects the cultural basis of such interaction in the social structure of our society. The notion of linkage is defined in rational-utilitarian terms and is devoid of cultural content. It is evident also from an assumption in this thesis that local mobilizations enjoy total autonomy or that they have a *sui generis* existence. Moreover, this view on Indian nationalism overemphasises particularistic manifestations of social and cultural forces denying pan-Indian national consciousness. Its 'collaborationist' notion of linkages between mass movements and British imperial administration, unconsciously promotes a 'pupil's progress' model of nationalism in India. The structural dissociation between the mass and the elite levels of national movements in this thesis is extended into a dichotomy between Eastern and Western social and cultural systems, and ideologies of nationalism.

This view abounds in the writing of several scholars on political culture and political system in contemporary India. Focus is on 'factional' characteristics of Indian political culture, its roots are primordial principles such as caste, kinship and religion. The segmentary features of society are enlarged as if these were the general principles of Indian social organisation and its cultural pattern. The particularistic features are universalised without taking into consideration social institutions which serve as links between local and national levels of functioning. Despite there being some awareness of limitations of such approach to understanding processes in Indian society, the tendency to hold to these views continues.

It is true that social institutions and groups at local levels in India enjoyed autonomy from elite traditions, but this autonomy was *relative*. Indian society through ages provided for organic linkages of these micro-institutions with the macro-organisations, such as economy, civilization, polity and administrative institutions. The dichotomy as posed between 'vertical' or elite levels of social and political mobilization and 'horizontal' or mass levels was not absolute. For example, horizontal mobilization of caste on vertical lines into 'caste association' used to take place long before Independence. The tribes differentiated into caste-like social formations. Even the comprehension of caste distinctions through ritual purity and pollution would have been impossible without a civilizational model of 'varna' with a pan-Indian extension of meanings and symbols. Otherwise, caste is only a regional entity. Comparative studies of folk cultures in geographically disparate regions show extensive commonalities of symbols, meanings and cultural contents across regions.

We might reiterate the historical role played by inter-structural autonomy of basic social institutions in Indian society. The institutions of social stratification, political administration and values and beliefs in their relative autonomy provided flexibility of responses to forces encroaching upon from the outside. These could be forces of colonialism, alien cultural contacts or contemporary processes of modernization. This relative autonomy of basic social institutions continues even today, but its quality is undergoing fast transformation. In traditional India, caste panchayats could in large measure conduct internal self-administration, avoid appeals to state administration for judicial settlements, since caste enjoyed stability and strength with support from other institutions such as economy, technology and belief systems. Yet, in the past also these regional cultural traditions had a sustained and institutionalised interaction with pan-Indian institutions. Professor N.K. Bose in his study of the geographical background of Indian culture, identifies several such institutions which provided linkages between local and national institutions in the past; these include: travelling mendicants, traders, story-tellers, craftsmen and artists. They came from all castes, low and high. The pilgrimage centres, fairs and festivals provided yet another nodal points of such interlinkages. Professor Bose concludes: 'Although India was, by and large illiterate, yet there were built up certain mechanisms by means of which common intellectual and emotional elements of culture were brought to the door of the most distant communities, isolated either by geography or the promotion of social separatism' (Bose: N.K.: 1977:6).

The autonomy of grass-root social institutions has been over-played in total disregard of linkages among these also as a device to under-rate the forces of unity in the Indian society and its civilization possibly as a measure of colonial or imperial policy of the British administrator-turned social scientists. In such writings, concepts such as 'caste', 'tribe', 'village', 'community', 'family and kinship' were defined as segmentary entities, often analogous to their socio-historical equivalents in the European society. The emphasis was on showing how each of these entities affirmed the principle of segmentation and autonomy rather than being parts of an organic whole. The element of discreteness was over-emphasised and the linkages, both social and cultural, which bound these entitles into an organic system of social structure and civilization were neglected' (Singh, Y: 1986: 1).

Localism and nationalism are social processes in continual interaction in all societies that have passed beyond the elementary stages of segmentary social organisation to civilization. This stage of societal evolution is achieved through advancement of civilization, a long drawn process of growth in economy, technology, political institutions and intellectual and artistic creativity. A civilization society has to build up linkages with local or mass level institutions, and communities to sustain itself economically, technologically and ideologically. Nationalism is a process, a product of historical conjuncture of social forces through which the linkages are not only established or expanded but also qualitatively strengthened. Nationalism is, therefore, not a finished product, nor a formal structure or normative model but an organic historical process through which civilization societies strengthen themselves by qualitative differentiation from within and their superior integration organically, within a territorial boundary. Often it is the formal notion of nationalism and its ideology that turns it into a monstrosity that all civilized societies must avoid. Nationalism as a social process evolves towards maturation as Louis Dumont suggests: 'nationalism refers to the nation as a tendency inspired by its existence or as the aspiration to build up a nation' (Louis Dumont: 1976:47).

For nationalism as a process, aspiration is as important as achievement. The studies on France, the first European nation, show that movement from provincialism to nationalism was often a fractured and painful process. In 1864 an inspector of education, touring the mountains of the Lozere, asked the children at a village school: 'In what country is Lozere situated?' Not a single pupil knew the answer. 'Are you English or Russian?', he demanded. They could not say. This was in one of the remoter parts of France, but the incident illustrates how Frenchmen gradually became aware of what it was that distinguished them from other men. The French nation had to be created' (Zeldin Theodore: 1980:3). Eighty three years later, in 1951, an opinion poll revealed the persistent hold of provincialism, and ambivalence towards the culture of the capital 'Paris' was strong. Only 42 per cent of the provincials (as opposed to 79 per cent of Parisians) knew who J.P. Sartre was—others described him variously as a street, a deputy, a painter and a dress designer' (quoted in Zeldin T: 1980:3). A publication in 1934 about France said that 'the clan and tribe still survive in small towns and in the countryside... People entrenched themselves in their little properties with their petty interests, and petty grievances ... mistrustful of young talent ... oblivious of the great problems of the world' (Ch. J. Million: 1934; quoted in Zeldin T: 1980:34).

Without indepth sociological historiography the western nationalism has come to present itself as a mythical model for Indian society and its many scholars. As deeper studies of its nationalism and national identity become available one gets more realistic assessment of the questions of nationalism and national identity. Writing in a publication of 1979 on France, Theodore Zeldin says: 'When I examine the forces working for the creation of more uniformity and unity in the country, I find the growth of a sense of national identity to be superficial, despite the imposition or adoption of a common language, and of common ways of thinking and talking which seem to distinguish Frenchmen from all other people (Zeldin Theodore: 1979: viii). According to Zeldin, French national identity is the creation of classes and politicians. It was reinforced by the policy of education and the existence of army. Not class struggle but urge for social mobility, competitiveness and anxiety dominated the personal behaviour of the people in this process. Zeldin notes how: 'By 1966 less than half (44-47 per cent) of metal workers in large factories said that for them the capitalist was the enemy; in small firms only 12-15 per cent held that view (Zeldin T: 1979: xi).

We have made these references not to pass value judgment on provincialism or nationalism but to illustrate that movement towards nationalism in any society is a process in which counterpulls of antagonistic tendencies remain active in accordance with. the conjuncture of historical and social forces. Humans get their maximum succour from their private life world and primordial ties. Hence nationalism should not mean in any society the total abolition or death of regional or provincial cultures or group identities. Our hypothesis is that neither the structure nor the normative construct of society could offer us sufficient measure of nationalism in a country. Its strength, more latent than manifest, lies in the linkages that bind these structures and norms at various levels into a super-organic whole which has great plasticity and, therefore, endurance. The movement from particularistic ties of *loyalty* to principles of nationalism and national identity is governed by emergence of social forces that trigger the process of modernization.

A modernization hypothesis is probably implicit in most debates on nationalism in developing societies. The relevant question is whether the model of modernization in terms of which nationalism in these societies is analysed is itself adequate or not. Most western models of modernization suffer from culturological fallacy, and historical analogues are proposed from western experiences without much regard for differences in basic values, history and social structure. Professor I.P. Desai made a perceptive remark in this context when he said that 'we should see the work of academicians abroad in terms of its relevance to what we are thinking and doing. It should not be other way round as it has been in the past' (Desai I.P.: 1981: 56).

Most Indian academicians we find today are sensitive to this question. They have continually endeavoured to formulate conceptual and theoretical responses to this problem. The dilemma they face is about evolving a conceptual frame through which complex linkages between nationalism and modernization in India, that are grounded empirically in primordial and provincial structures and values, could be explained through universalistic concepts and categories that are also sensitive to historical specificity of the Indian process of nationalism. In simple terms, the question is: can tradition be modernized? Or, would the 'cunning of reason', the Enlightenment ideology of which nationalism is an off-shoot ultimately triumph and imprison nationalism in the iron cage of universal history? To many scholars both in India and abroad answer to this question poses crucial problems of nationalism and modernization. A large number of them, however, postulate opposition between tradition and modernity and between provincialism and nationalism, as conceptual dichotomies. Our contention is that tradition, modernity, or provincialism, nationalism should not be seen as reified normative structures but as social processes. The impregnable wall that isolates and divides them is *semantic* not *real*.

The structuralist theory in sociology and social sciences has encouraged the tendency among both the marxist and non-rnarxist scholars to postulate social, economic and cultural parameters of nationalism, modernization and development, etc. in logical sets of opposites or in binary terms, where linkages between them are tenuous not real, syntactical not historical. Consequently, analysis of nationalism under such theoretical impulses fore-closes the possibilities of constructive reciprocity and interaction between tradition and modernity, between nationalism and provincialism and between equality and hierarchy. Louis Dumont in his treatment of questions of communalism and nationalism in India articulates this dilemma when he says that in India, 'elements such as people and territory, normatively stressed on one side, are found as *empirical and undifferentiated datum* on the other. The orientation to ultimate values shows a more drastic and complex difference. On the traditional side, the ultimate values. are found in the conformity of each element to the role assigned to it in the whole of being as such. In the modern society, they are found in the concrete human indivisible element, which is taken as an end in itself, and as the source of all norms, rationality and order; in other words, the Individual. As history shows transition is difficult, and has given rise to intermediary forms' (Dumont L: 1964: 70). Louis Dumont recognises the significances of *interaction* between tradition and nationalism or even the existence of intermediary forms. His doubt about a smooth or even successful transition to nationalism in traditional societies is based on the diversity of the two worldviews one hierarchical, that is Indian and the other individualistic, that is western, of which nationalism and modernization are products.

One might easily notice elements of historicity and formalism in the views expressed by Dumont and others who approach the question of nationalism as opposition between tradition and modernity. In operational terms, this opposition exists in the dualism of what is defined as 'rational' and 'basic' or fundamental in the value system of societies. Indian society. is supposed to be rooted in fundamental value system of hierarchy, and its transition to nationalism or modernization is thwarted due to lack of primacy of rational values in social life. The limitation of this reasoning rests in its non-recognition of the fact that in real life rational values have a tendency to co-exist with basic or fundamental values. The social, political and economic processes of change in India illustrate this fact. The challenge in India is not of the transition from tradition to modernity but of the modernization of Indian tradition.

Historical experience of nationalism even in the western societies shows that crucial factors which contributed to institutionalisation of nationalism and to their modernization were primarily through rational technological changes. The basic values or the religious worldview of western society only accommodated these transformations. The growth of one has not led to the obsolescence of the other. The relevant question, however, which makes a material difference between successful or not so successful transition to modernization of which nationalism is a historical by-product is how successfully rational principles are applied for the growth of society.

The Indian experience in this context dearly indicates

that rational values have been widely imbibed in the uses of technology in public and private life: All sections of people covet for careers in sciences and professions. Pragmatism in political, economic and social life, is widely pursued, often outcrossing limits of principles or moral standards. In practical life, be it agriculture, trade, industry, transport or other services, adoption of modern utilitarian or rational values is common. So, if measures of nationalism and modernization are acceptance of rational values, Indian society is well on the way to this goal. These values, however, co-exist with traditional basic values and worldview. Instead of replacement there is adaptive synthesis of the rational with the traditional values and beliefs. Largely, this is how it should be. But this process of adaptive change sets into motion also counter-tendencies or negative social forces which not only serve as impediments to modernization but also threaten the processes of nationalism and national integration.

These counter-tendencies emerge from the sharpening consciousness of social and economic inequalities among groups in society. Modernization has set into motion a process of social restructuration in our society. The traditional society was based on a relative evenness in the dimensions of social, economic and political status of people at an integrated, though lower level of social order. The rational and basic values of society were integrated together due to relative stability of the former, represented pre-eminently by technology. The process of modernization upsets this balance in society. The rational or utilitarian values not only far outweigh the basic moral values of society, but expand faster and have higher degree of intensity. This coincides with emergence of high information society. In India, political participation, mass media, education, social mobility and increasing incidence of migration have intensified the awareness of social and economic inequalities. Continuous inculcation of values of consumerism and ostentatious life style of privileged sections has negative effect upon people in general. The modern means of communication make consciousness of social inequalities carry sharper edge which distorts the perception of a rational order of society. This creates imbalance in the means-end relationship in the pursuits of life chances.

Violence, communalism, casteism and regionalism erupt symbolising these distortions in means-end relationship in pursuits of social, economic, political and cultural objectives. The process of modernization enlarges opportunities which adds to the strength of the middle classes, professional groups and political functionaries. These new classes are products of social restructuration and social mobility. A substantial segment of these new classes climbs to higher status through dysnomic pathways. Ironically, this process also creates pauperization in rural areas, marginalization of peasantry and urban migration of the rural poor. Not all the underprivileged people that emerge in this process have subaltern identity, as not all new social climbers have commitment to rational utilitarian ethos. We witness all over the country today this process, where resentment of underprivileged is coming face to face with cussedness and arrogance of the dominant classes. Provincialism and commualism are products of this environment. If the emergence of new middle classes consolidates the processes of Indian nationalism by widening and strengthening the societal linkages in the system, the linkages of territory, administration, resources, market, technology and culture; it is also sharpening the divide between privileged and underprivileged that reinforces tendencies towards communalism, regionalism and counter-nationalism. The Constitution of our republic does not envisage only legal rational order. It encompasses it in the basic values of socialism, secularism arid democracy. Strengthening linkages in the social system sponsored by the needs of the dominant classes in society may not achieve these goals, and may lead to fractured modernization. History tells us, to be wary of nationalism that is a product of such process. It leads to brutal application of state power for repression of underprivileged in society. Solution lies in a model of modernization that is consensual and aims at vigorous pursuit of goals of social justice in society. This alone will strengthen the roots of nationalism in our society.

REFERENCES

Bose, N.K.: *Culture and Society in India,* New Delhi: Asia Publishing House, 1977.

Chandra, Bipan: *The Rise and Growth of Economic Nationalism in India,* Delhi: People's Publishing House, 1966.

Nationalism and Colonialism in Modem India, New Delhi: Orient Longman, 1981.

Desai, A.R.: *Social Background of Indian Nationalism,* Bombay, Oxford University Press, 1948.

Desai, J.P.: *The Craft of Sociology and Other Essays,* Delhi: Ajanta Publications, 1981.

Chatterjee, Partha: *Nationalist Thought and the Colonial World: A Derivative Discourse,* Delhi: Oxford University Press, 1986.

Dumont, Louis: 'Nationalism and Communalism', *Contributions to Indian Sociology,* Paris: Mouton and Co., 1964.

Guha, Ranjit (ed.) *Subaltern Studies* I, Delhi: Oxford University Press, 1982.

Seal, Anil: 'Imperialism and Nationalism in India', in (eds) John Gallagher, Gordon Johnson and Anil Seal, *Locality, Province and Nation: Essays on Indian Politics* 1870 to 1940, Cambridge University Press, 1973.

Yogendra Singh: 'Indian Sociology', *Current Sociology,* Vol. 34, No. 2, 1986.

Zeldin Theodore: France 1848-1945: *Politics and Anger* New York: Oxford University Press, 1979.

Zeldin Theodore: France 1848-1945: *Intellect and Pride,* New York: Oxford University Press, 1980.

Chapter 10

National Integration in Indian Society

The perspective in which the issue of national integration and development confronts us today is qualitatively different. In the 1950's, the problem was primarily of institutionalisation of the values, the ideas and the institutions of nationhood for which supposedly we had little to draw from our past. We faced the dilemma of an "old society and new state." We were confronted with the anxieties of economic and industrial growth; the looming food shortage, ascending demands from regional, caste, communal and linguistic interest groups cast a dark spell on the national horizon. The memories of partition were still fresh. The experiment in adult franchise and democratic institution-building was itself new, and comparisons with the Western democracies revealed fewer parallels to reinforce our morale. Despite Nehru's overwhelming presence on the national scence, the doubts about successful institution of democratic polity in India continued in the evocation of anxiety as to 'after Nehru what'? There was continual eruption of tensions rooted in varied forms of primodialities threatening the civic principles of nation-building.

In the 1980's today, the issues of national integration could be reviewed both in prospect and retrospect. The context of development now accords new weightage to the evaluation of our social problems. The issues of value integration have not undergone basic changes but their intrinsic character and context have indeed undergone qualitative transformation. Thirty-five years of experiences, hopeful as well as painful, of successes as well as of failures offer us today a new backdrop of events in which a more predictable and mature view of the problems of value integration could be taken. The notion of development in this matrix of analysis serves both as an ideology and indicator of value integration.

Ideology of Value Integration

The ideology of value integration has been viewed by social scientists in India in a variety of ways. The outstanding variations are those of the systemic and processual approaches. Both these view also inhere philosophical presuppositions about the construction of social reality. The systemic view is most prominent and conforms to the dominant orientation in social science methodology and theory. It views the process of development and value. integration in a society in terms of its logical congruence with a set of abstract attributes of a selected systemic forms, such as feudalism, capitalism, colonialism and socialism, etc., and future social changes or their outcome are accorded value on a formal basis of generalisation. The students of contemporary period have considerable literature available on development and value integration and one is familiar with such orientation in reasoning. Debates have recently drawn attention to the contradictions crystallised or emerging ones in India which threaten the processes of development and value integration, or distort the processes of development. The class character of the state and society in India, their hegemonistic role in the processes of industrialisation, and agrarian growth, the feudalistic syndrome in political culture and its craft, the persistence of feudatory ethos in bureaucratic rationality under the overarching umbrella of parasitic and often neocolonial psyche of the ruling elite are quoted as indicators of the contradictions in the process of development and value integration.

There is much to commend in this systemic appraisal of the ideology of development and value integration. It contributes richly to formalisation of method, theoretic neatness and richness of generalisations. It, however, suffers from fallacies of over abstraction, lack of reflexivity in the grasp of the import of events and the neglect of the historicity of social structures and traditions. In the Indian setting the role of caste as opposed to materialist rationality and of locality as opposed to cosmopolitanism are some of the initial historical conditions which have continued to deeply influence the processes of development and social change. These, however, do not fit neatly into the models of systemic formulation of development and value integration ideology. Marxist theory, among the systemic varieties of theory, offers possibilities of going beyond the formalism of approach. Ironically, however, this too, among the many models of the evaluation of Indian processes of development and value integration has shown the tendency towards formalisation. The notion of dialectics which gives Marxist theory a special advantage in going to the-*roots of the social processes* in the historicity of their setting for the understanding of social changes has most often been relegated into the background under the zealous attempts towards system formulation.

An alternative strategy of explanation of the ideology of development and value integration is to begin from the focus on social processes. The dialectical reasoning offers explanations regarding development and value integration. Instead of beginning from the system formulations deductively, emphasis here shifts to the observation of social processes with projection of systemic forms in a retroductive fashion. The methodology here is not deductive but retroductive, not formal but reflexive, not abstract but historical. This approach also overcomes the anomalies of orchestration of factual inconsistencies into system forms which abound in formalistic theorising about the Indian society. In operational terms, the dialectical approach draws richly from the logical power of many theoretic structures in social sciences both Marxist and non-marxist without, however, implying a deductive system constraint.

The theme of nation-building in the political theory of development offers a processual approach which we Witness in the writings of Karl Duetsch, G. Almond, S. Verba, Lucien Pye and others. Emphasis here is on the growth of certain processes such as political socialisation, political participation, interest articulation, interest aggregation, political recruitment, rule making, rule application and rule adjudication, etc. These are treated as essential components of the forces of nation-building and political development. A number of Indian political scientists have also followed this model in their analysis of our political institutions. The political development theory of national integration no doubt offers us an example of the processual approach. The serious limitation that it suffers from is its lack of historicity. It implicitly assumes a universal model of nation-building in the mirror image of the western, mainly American democracy. The process categories that it formulates for analysis of development are ethnocentric and grounded into the assumptions of consesuality typical of a functional theory. It is completely devoid of the notion of dialectics.

The paradoxes that the application of this theory on the processes of development in India have revealed are many. such as, political participation Without political socialisation, rule-making without rule application and political recruitment without interest articulation. At the root of these seeming paradoxes lies. the historicity of the Indian tradition and social structure. This indeed could not be anticipated by the political development theory, which tends to be mystified by formalism of categories.

In the formulation of the 'process categories' for the undertaking of the basic problems of national integration and development in India one needs to focus on dialectics and history. The dialectical view of social reality offers the potential for understanding the social forces in the process 'of their evolutionary unfoldment, the contradictions to which they culminate, the social dimensions of these contradictions and the possibilities of their reconciliation or revolutionary transformation. The contexts of these possibilities is conditioned by historicity of the social processes. This approach implies a cognitive reflexivity in the craft of the social scientist, to empathise with the events, I with the crossmirroring of experiences within himself and in the members of the society at large through which alone a critical social theory of development is possible.

So far we have raised the methodological question on the ideology of development and value integration. We could now outline some of its concrete parameters. These have initially been enshrined in the Constitution of India and operationalised by numerous policy statements, five year plans and other documents of national policy on social, economic and cultural transformation of our society. All these declarations add up to the futuristic perspective of a society that we wish to establish. It does not bear a clear cut systemic formulation. It is conveyed through the phrase "socialistic pattern of society", in which the values of democracy, secularism and socialism are predominant. These values could better be understood as indicators of social processes which the state wishes to augment and maximise, through a series of measures of social, economic, political and cultural reforms. The constitution aims at establishing an equalitarian democratic society based on cultural pluralism, secularism, a composite culture, rule of law based on the principles of civic society through a federal polity. A series of fundamental rights are instituted in the constitution for the citizens of the state to invoke their freedom and the Directive Principles of the state policy enshrine some of the collective values that the state must pursue for achieving cultural, economic and ethical objectives commensurate with the ideals laid down.

The pattern of integration that the nation ultimately aims at achieving is that of a civic society with a balanced proportion of individual freedom and social responsibility, of cultural pluralism and a national composite culture of secularism, liberalism and scientific ethos with the continuity of the valued aspects of the past tradition. It aims at progressive social differentiation, characteristic of a modern society with emphasis on equalitarianism and social justice. The mechanism to achieve these goals are twofold: acceleration of opportunities for upward social mobility and positive discrimination in favour of the traditionally exploited sections of society. The first strategy is the classical process of social changes in all capitalist societies, but the latter element defies the ideal type of a liberal capitalist path and adds a new element to our social policy. It is this element in the India's strategy for development which does not clearly fit our policy and patterns of social transformation into neat systemic typologies. The strategy to achieve the measure of social growth with social justice is thus largely capitalist-liberal with deliberate state intervention into sensitive and needy sectors of society which require protective treatment to move upward in the process of social mobility.

The structural elements of national integration which constitute part of this process of differentiation and integration in our body politic are federal organisation of state, competitive structure of political parties, special rights of minorities, scheduled caste, scheduled tribes, and other deprived sections of society such as women and backward classes, etc. Value integration involves organic development of all these segments of our life through differentiation and evolution in society.

Development and Value Integration

The challenges to value integration in the 1950's were

from forces that could be termed as that of structuration. Each segment in the national body politic desired to ensure for itself a path of opportunities for development ,and a share in the national resources, wealth and power. The outline of the issues of integration painted by Selig Harrison and other students of this problem in the 1950's brings out this phenomenon clearly. Issues of language, minority politics in the Punjab and the southern states or among the tribal states in eastern India, the demands from the scheduled castes, tribes and other deprived sections of the society, were couched in the matrix of new expectations. The entire movement had a futuristic orientation in a nascent body politic in which hopes and aspirations had been roused and promises made to lay down the foundation of a modern democratic state. It was enough in such a scheme of things to contain the interest articulation by formal means of policy planning, waiting yet for the substantive results. The coordinates of value integration at this stage were formal and structural. Demands generated by the interest groups were anchored in institutional innovations, rule-making and contractual promises, rather than immediate rewards. The latter was already supposed to have been initiated through the measures of, the land reforms, abolition of jagirdari and zamindari, establishment of the panchayati raj and the new industrial and economic policies. The adaptive nature of the linguistic policy, the reorganisation of states, non-interferences in the personal laws of the religious minorities and safeguarding of their educational and cultural institutions, the reservation of constituencies for the SC and ST and assurances of favoured socio-economic dealing to them could contain the centrifugal pulls within the framework of formal policies. The freshness of new earned freedom and the tradition of national movement also contributed to the mutuality of idealistic orientation among the contending interest groups.

The futuristic character of the issues in value integration of the 1950's has today assumed a retrospective overtone. Today, the interest groups, be they minorities, SC or ST, backward classes or corporate bodies such as the Centre and the state (relationships) look back at the records of the promises kept during the years since independence. The new perspective of this problem is rooted basically in the social dialectics of the past decades. It would be necessary to evaluate the developmental processes which have got enmeshed with the issues of national integration. There have been many developments during the past decades which bear directly upon the structural issues of national integration. Expansion of science and technology into the far flung rural areas has contributed to what is called green revolution. It has led to far reaching sociological consequences; such as the consolidation of the power base of the middle castes with substantial numerical dominance, the decline of the feudal aristocracy, sharpening of the caste and class contradictions in the villages, the confrontation of the middle castes with the Harijans and landless labourers. There has been an ascendancy of youth-power in the social, economic and political life, partly due to the fast rate of population growth but mainly due to the spread of technology and its associated institutions in the. developmental processes. The rural segment has emerged as a significant power base in the national politics as is evident in the peasant trade unionism and farmers lobby. The emergence of the middle castes in the villages as a powerful economic and political class has sharpened the conflicts between them and lower castes on the one hand, , and on the other, has led to the introduction of new political demands and styles. This pattern is common throughout the country; the Jats, Ahirs, Kurmis in the. north, the Patels, Kunbis and Marathas in the west and the Reddys; Kammas and Vokaliggas in the south set 'a uniform profile of middle caste socio-economic ascendancy and new structural tensions.

This development has given caste a new role in the national integration. The substantial numerical size of these middle castes and their horizontal dispersal throughout the region has contributed to their political clout. The emergence of the backward class movement epitomises this process. These movements which began as social reform enterprises with nuances of sanskritization in the past, have increasingly assued political character. The institution of the Mandal Commission for reservation of jobs for the backward classes reflects how these demands have had strong appeal in political circles. The MandaI Commission has recommended reservation of jobs to the tune of 27 percent for the backward classes which constitute according to its estimates about 52 percent of population in India. Indeed it argues in favour of reservation to the tune of 52 per cent but only due to the Supreme Court ruling that reservation at a time should not exceed 50 percent it opts for the 27 percent level. This recommendation is indeed symptomatic of the strength that caste consciousness has assumed in the realm of public policy.

Apart from the rearticulation of caste consciousness and caste identity in the rural cultural and political life a new vista that development has added to it is that of greater politicalisation and media exposure of the rural population, particularly the youth. Following the declaration of the emergency in 1975, a new qualitative change in the social psychology of youth and their political images has come about. A new political culture which is more sensitive to ends rather than means and exudes a sense of cynicism and disenchament about most issues of national life has taken place. This negative development contributes to the deterioration of the law and order situation and the erosion of institutional cannons of a civic society. It has, however, led also to some positive results. The increased political awareness has rendered the rural electorate impervious to appeal through mere primordiality. The analysis of electoral data shows healthy trend in voting behaviour; within the framework of caste and regional identities which no doubt provide the matrix for the electoral appeal, political performance is one of the major criteria for electoral support. The pulls of charisma and primordiality are defined within the limits of political performance.

The social and economic development has also thrown up new issues in the national integration of the scheduled caste in our social and cultural life. The policy of job reservation, and other elements of positive discrimination during the past decades have happily created a small segment of middle-class among the scheduled castes. In a milieu of increased caste consciousness the demonstration effect of this group over the other castes in the urban areas and among the white collar professional categories has been negative. It has already led to caste riots in Gujarat and other parts of the country. There is a nexus here between development and tensions of integration. As the level of education among the scheduled caste increases, it leads to greater politicalization of the youth and other members of this community. New ideological rationalisation, is sought to carry forward their movement. Conversion to Islam is the latest expression of this process. It highlights, on the one hand, the sharpening contradictions between the upper caste and the scheduled caste relationship and on the other, brings the issue of social mobility of the scheduled caste in the arena of communal politics, a sensitive aspect of our body politic.

This ideological orientation in the scheduled caste movement is linked closely with the processes of economic and social development. The alienation of a large section of the scheduled caste, especially in the villages from the outcome of economic development, their continual persecution by the rich rural peasantry coupled with S.C.'s greater political awareness and internal cohesion spurs the radicalisation of their movement. The same process also prevails in the urban areas. In contradistinction to this, the upper and middle caste professional and white collar workers in small towns and cities feel that the measure of protective discrimination for the SC have been detrimental to their own interests as also to the universalistic values of merit, and achievement. This feeling seems to have gained more ground recently leading to the reciprocal alienation and hostility between the SC and the caste Hindus. It is a new phenomenon which did not exist in the 1950's when there was high degree of national consensus on this issue. The reason for this cleavage in the social psychology of the two castes lies in the process of social mobility and change in the economic structure of their relationship.

The studies of social stratification in India clearly highlight the emergence of a new middle caste as a powerful socio-economic group in the rural areas. But these studies also bring out the incidences of upper caste pauperisation, especially from among the section of the former landlords and priestly castes. This together with narrowing of the opportunities for employment in the white collar and professional jobs had added to the discomfiture of the upper and middle castes. The social psychology against reservation is further reinforced by the demand from other backward classes, etc. for similar job reservation, which indeed have been implemented in most state level services. This in totality adds up to a latent class struggle in the rural and urban areas in India in the guise of caste tensions. The effort to rationalise this conflict through ideological discussion on the role of merit versus need in employment policy is besides the point. The main question that Indian polity faces today is not that of the first principles but of the strategies of consensus making within the framework of limited resources, and widening demands.

The place of tribes in national integration, though structurally similar in socio-economic mobility to that of caste has yet been historically and politically of a different nature. This is particularly so in the states and the union territories in eastern India. Here the tribal social structure has historically enjoyed a cultural and social homogeneity and autonomy quiet different from the tribes in the mainland country, say in West Bengal, Bihar, Orissa, M.P. and southern states of Karnataka and Andhra Pradesh. The mainland tribal structure due to closer interaction with caste strata had reached a higher level of status differentiation and got enmeshed into tribe-caste relationship of political and economic exploitation within the framework of hierarchy. This is evident in the tribal movement against the *dikus* in Bihar and the merchant caste expropriators in Orissa and other parts of central India. In the north-eastern part, the tribal problem of national integration is linked with the peculiarities of the segmentary organisation of the tribes on the one hand, which determines their age-old internal equation of relationships and on the other, it is tied with the political issues of federalism, decentralisation of political power and socio-economic reforms. Issues of an extraneous kind also intervene in this process given the tradition of these tribes and their social structure. A common pattern which one might discern in the relationship of tribes and national integration in general is anchored on the insider-outsider syndrome in which the outsider is either a specific nontribal caste or class or the apparatus of the state which is. identified as the symbol of exploitation. Most recent tribal agitations have, therefore, had a semblance of class conflict in one case or insurgency in another but structurally speaking, their sociological roots are common. A positive response obviously lies in confidence building backed by socio-economic measures of reform which contribute to the cessation of exploitation.

The development that has taken place both in the social and economic life of the scheduled castes and tribes in India as a result of the measures of reform and investment have led to an internal differentation within their social .structure. The base of better-to-do families amongst them has today widened, there are more educated persons amidst them than in the past, their socio-political awareness has gone up and corresponding to it the intensity of their identity consciousness has also soared. In this light, a new internal dialectics has begun to operate within their social structure; a homogeneous nondifferentied community has got class differentied, has thrown up class leadership which sponsors movements. This is the fruit of efforts towards social and economic development and a natural precursor to further growth, given the fact that this dialectics is understood and a flexible and consensual response is made to manage this dynamics of social change.

The issues of national integration are also vitally located in the changing perception of religious, linguistic and regional consciousness. These too have undergone changes in the process of development. The changes have come about first, due to alteration in the social structure of these communities as also due to changes in the political culture and social motion of our society. Compared to the 1950's, the social mobility and economic development among the Muslims in India, has shown a remarkable growth. Studies, however, indicate that in comparison to the north Indian Muslims, those in the southern part have done better economically and occupationally. This has augmented their self-confidence and organically linked them further with our socio-political and cultural fabric. It has contributed positively to the emergence of a composite culture. But this has also let lose an economic competition and inter-class strifes which take a communal colour due to negative value associations of the past. Thus, the false consciousness of communalism in India is exposed, but the nation has not yet fully succeeded in its de-mystification. The process of development has given a new context to the minority consciousness which remains sensitive and calls for a consensual approach. The crucial role in this process is to be played by the political parties and elite. The colonial anchorage of the ideology of communalism is slowly eroding but the new support from a positive political culture that is required for its containment has not come about. On the contrary, political opportunism now takes the better of the interest of communal integration. This could be illustrated by a variety of intercommunal tensions. In a world environment of fundamentalist revival it is imperative that the issues of communalism, in any variety or form are tackled as matters of national consensus. In the tricky process of our electoral politics this has not been possible so far.

Communalism in its wider context constitutes the single most challenging problem to our national integration. The problems of tribe, caste, linguistic group, religious minorities, all of them could be seen arising from the contradictions of not only values but also economic and political interests which remain disguised in value-loaded ideological formulations, The process of development amongst the minorities and deprived categories has to some extent blunted the edge of communalism, but the process of political and economic competition that development has unleashed tends to reinforce communal identities in the form of new ideological resources for cooperative mobilisation and interest articulation. This would seem to be the new context in which communalism continues to have a sway in our national culture and inter-community relationship. If we examine closely, the movement for Khalistan, Assam agitation, Jharkhand movement, or other expressions of communal, linguistic and religious dissent in our polity, all of them share underlying structural impulses that are anchored in anxieties about the share in power or economic resources.

The role of the international geo-politics must be recognised but cannot be taken as the central causal force in most such movements. Indeed, these movements deserve empathic understanding and structural response rather than an emotive or repressive treatment.

Political Culture and National Integration

The process of development has contributed to several contradictory pulls in the cultural profile of our nation. There has been a rise in entrepreneurial ethos both in industry and agriculture; people have positively responded to science and technology as instruments of economic and social reconstruction; media exposure and level of social awareness of all sections of our society has risen very high; there is evidence of an all round, high level of psychic mobility in instrumental walks of life. These developments have, however, not replaced age old traditionalism, religiosity and pulls towards down-right obscurantism. This contradiction compounds the problems of national integration.

Here, we face some of the most disappointing tendencies. The culture and style of our political elite has progressively become non-cosmopolitan and capricious. Its demonstration effect on the youth and public tends to be negative and promotes delegitimation of cherished institutional values. No single political party could be named as being individually responsible, as the malady seems to be all pervasive and near total. The contradictory pulls of cosmpolitanism and localism are no doubt a universal feature of all political systems, especially democracies. But the political culture though responding to local demands does not in most cases consciously promotes localism or primordiality. In India, due to the peculiarities of its social structure and the universal predominance of caste and ethnic ties, the primordial structures have adduced to themselves even the formal roles in political, economic and other institutional settings. The national ideology in India should not legitimate primorality at the formal level, and attempt to contain it at the substantive level. This has not taken place, however.

The political party system in India has considerably weakened, its institutional structures have been bypassed by party leadership itself. No doubt, personal influence and charisma have played a very significant role in political parties in India. But its contribution to the stable growth of the political system cannot remain outside the matrix of institutional structures or organisation. If it does so charisma may turn into prophecy and lead to high fluidity of the political system and give rise to nonrational tendencies. It is the conformity to a set of institutional norms that gives predictability and accountability to political systems and lends them a measure of rationality. Democracy epitomises this process as distinct from feudalism or patrimonialism. It is strengthened only though rational party organisation.

The evidence so far in this area is negative. There has been a rise of opportunism and factionalism in our political culture. Politics by its very nature is to a large extent factious, but it is the ideological foundation of these factions that determines the measure of their negative or positive role. In our context, it appears that negative context has been higher and seems to have crossed beyond the quotient of toleration for the system as a whole. It is imperative that political parties and political elite closely review this aspect of our political culture and evolve mechanism for its correction.

We may conclude by saying that the sociological forces in our country today present both positive and negative tendencies in the sphere of national integration. There are remarkable indicators of growth and development in our economic, cultural and political life. In political realm the voters response at the hustings has been remarkably substantial belying many predictions that democracy will not succeed in India. The people have responded remarkably though the same can hardly be said about our politicians and elite. The growth in agricultural and industrial entrepreneurship has been very substantial confirming the place that techno-economic rationality has now carved for itself in our daily life. It has, however, not done so at the cost of people's roots in their past or their tradition. The picture of change in India still suggests the continuation of the urge to accommodate and synthesise. Thus, many traditional institutions such as religion, joint family, caste and kinship which were supposed to be non-conducive to the process of modernization, have not thwarted its growth. The process of development on the other hand, has enlarged and intensified the class contradictions in our society. The goal of socialism or establishment of a just society has not been reached. The gap in this regard remains as large as ever, if not more. It is this contradiction on the one hand, and on the other the deterioration in our political culture and its ethos which has lent strength to forces of localism and primordiality as against cosmopolitanism and nationality. This under-development in the process of our development contributes to the perpetuation as well as revival of tendencies nonconducive to national integration.

Any process in our country which goes to reduce the pace of our march towards a socialist or just society, compromises the degree of consensuality in our body politic and becomes a burden on our goal towards national, integration. The more we accelerate this process along with economic growth the more we strengthen the institutional foci of national integration.

Chapter 11

Concept of Social Structure

Concept of social structure is entwined with the status of social theory. The recent years in sociology have, on the one hand, revealed the crisis in theory, and on the other hand, have indicated the tendencies toward theoretical convergence. Both these tendencies have deeply been implicated in the understanding of the concept of social structure. The crisis in theory is reflected in several forms: such as, the lack of nomological adequacy, or a theoretical nature of most sociological theories, fetishisation and reification of concepts, the muddle of metaphors in theorising, leading to multiplicity of paradigms in a single 'theory', together with its misplaced formalism and conscious, or sometimes unconscious, ideological mystification in the name of 'science' and 'objectivity'. The issues at the basis of this crisis mirror the foot steps of sociology, as well as its tasks ahead. As sociology gains deeper and deeper knowledge of social reality, as its conceptual and theoretical apparatus arc exposed 10 multiplicity of historical, social and cultural life-situations, as it faces up to the new challenges of change, its conceptual and theoretical repertoire are subjected to fresh validation. New operational demands emerge with changes in its meta-theoretical foundations.

System, Structure and Process

Among the sociological theories, functionalism contributed most to the understanding of social structure. It offered a principle, the notion of teleology through which the observed ensembles of social realities in concrete life-situations were rendered meaningful as an integrated system. The properties of the social structure were not only derived, but also understood through the notion of 'system', which was a construction and a logical explanatory device. This is revealed by the studies of social anthropologists which have offered indepth analysis of simpler societies. The notion of structure; however, was treated as real. For Radcliff Brown, Malinowski and Nadel, social structure is the 'order' of social relationships, roles and statutes which constitute the apparent reality and are outside human mind. With the exception of Malinowski to some extent, functionalism rejects representation of ensembles of social structure in human consciousness. It is treated non-psychologically, with the help of the notion of 'system' as a logical artifice. This is where the confusion in functionalist treatment of social structure starts. Social structure is real, and yet not real enough. It is an empirical fact, and yet a logical construction, sometimes statistical tableau, sometimes a kinship polygraph or a geological chart. Yet, its major fallacy is the assumption that what is apparent is real.

The formalism of the concept of social structure in functionalist theory begins from this logical ambiguity. The notion of system which it uses as a logical device, to give sense to the chaos of empirical ensembles of society, is in course of time reified. Its conceptual dynamism becomes the obverse of it—conceptual stasis. How did it come about? To answer this question, we have to examine the process of concept formation in functional sociology. The emphasis on induction, inference and facticity in funtionalist empiricism and its historicity, reduce concepts to attributional inventories, rather than a set of typical or patterned relationships. Such concepts are essentially nominal in nature and hardly inhere any propositions. George C. Homans, examining the notions of 'role', 'status' and 'institutions' in functionalist theory, brought out the *ad hoc* and random character of such concepts, which are devoid of any explanatory significance, save their generalised teleology. Those, who have later attempted to logically resurrect the functionalist notion of social structure, such as Carl Hempel and Naegel, have also recognised the severe limitations of teleology in the notion of social system. Most sociological concepts, such as 'group', 'community', 'castes', 'class', etc., which tend to describe social structure in functionalist idiom, constitute a set of attributes which internally have no logical relationships. Being neither transitive or exhaustive or exclusive, most these attributes defining key concepts of social structure lack power of generalisation and comparison. This is particularly true, in the areas of social, economic and power relationships. In the field of kinship and family studies, as we find in the writings of several social anthropologists, nominal concepts have been increasingly replaced by 'real' or propositional ones. In such cases we find teleology being replaced by causation, sometimes, materialistic, at other times, cultural. A dynamic and largely determinate relationship between infrastructure and superstructure is also introduced in most such analyses. Examples can be quoted from Durkheim, Radcliffe Brown, Malinowski, Murdock, Maurice Godelier and many others.

Contrary to more general impression popularised by Ralph Daharendorf, We do not think that major limitation of functionalist theory of social structure is its emphasis on 'consensus', or its neglect of 'conflict' in the social systems. No living society can remain in a state of perpetual consensus, and conflict does get resolved in most societies through orchestration of consensus. It is irrational to assume societies to be in states of permanent relationships of conflict or consensus. Moreover, prominent sociologists and social anthropologists have themselves used the notion of conflict in their treatment of social system from a functional perspective. Max Gluckman, Smelser, and in later works, Talcott Parsons and Coser, have made use of the process of conflict both to analyse the system-states as well as processes of social change and social movements. The essential limitation of functionalism and its notion of social structure is not its overemphasis on consensus or even neglect of dialectic of conflict. It lies in its poverty of theory, its artificial closure of concepts describing social structure, its poverty of explanatory mechanism and its fetishisation and reification of system-state. This leads to a mechanistic and static view of social reality. Functionalism suffers from these as it neglects history and the comprehension of reality as a process in the treatment of social structure. Its theoretical closure only generates opaque concepts that are self-explanatory and self-maintaining tautologies, and being devoid of history and sense of process these remain outside the ken of confirmation or disconfirmation through the panorama of human experience.

This tendency of which we accuse functionalism also prevails in the structuralist and a variety of neo-Marxist views of social structure. Godelier is right when he says: "There are two methodological principles, recognised by functionalism, structuralism, and Marxism alike, which are basic to the scientific study of social facts. The first stipulates that analysis of social relations must not be analysed in isolation, but considered in their reciprocal relationships—as entities forming 'systems'. The second stipulates that these systems must be analysed in their internal logic prior to analysing their genesis or evolution" (Godelier:1978:page 44). The tendency towards formalism, however, is shared also in common among functionalist, structuralist and structuralist-Marxist approaches. In the contributions of Levi Strauss, the leader of structuralist thought, one may find a place both for history and comparison. But as he treats social structure as a model, not observable directly, a set of social ensembles that attain 'order' through 'transformation' or possibilities of transformation, his notion of history remains universalised and abstract. It is visible from the studies of myth and kinship through which Levi Strauss has usually constructed his notion of social structure. His structural analysis, while not denying history, cannot go hand in hand with it, since it has separated the analysis of 'types' of kinship relations from the analysis of their 'functions'. These functions are neither ignored nor denied, but they are never explored for what they are. And so the question of any real articulation between kinship relations and other social structures which characterise historically determined, concrete societies, is never analysed: Levi Stauss confined himself to extracting from concrete facts a 'formal system' of kinship relations, a system which he then studies in its internal logic and compares with other types, either similar or different, but belonging even in their differences, to the same group of transformations" (Godelier M:48). Thus the fallacy of 'system-states' in functionalism is replaced in structuralism by the fallacy of 'orders' and 'transformations'.

This tendency is also discernible in Marxism, specially the neo-Marxism of the structuralist variety. A representative example of this variety is found in the contributions of Althusser, Lucien Goldmann and others. The Marxist notion of social structure and its theoretical formulation, which is otherwise much more wholesome and sound, has been rendered formal and sterile under such structuralist treatment. The notions of history, modes of production, dialectical process of transformation, class and social structure, ideology and alienation, which are, operational concepts in Marxism and add both objectivity and explanatory power to the theory are made vacuous and transcendent. Take Althusser 's concept of history: he draws a basic dissociation between theory of history and empirical history, and aims at "liberating the theory of history from any compromise with 'empirical temporality'. Similarly, to Althusser "The truth of history cannot be read in its manifest discourse, because the text of history is not a text in which a voice (the Logis) speaks but the inaudible and illegible notion of the effects of a structure of structures" (Reading Capital, [R.C.] in Thompson E.P. page 207). History is thus abstracted completely from concrete temporal experiences. It is in line with structuralist epistemology of Althusser which goes beyond historical materialism of Marx in the process caricaturing it in the image of neo-idealism. This is also reflected in his formulation of the concepts of social structure, infrastructure and superstructure, the concepts which in Marxist methodology are anchored into the notion of modes of production and their relationships.

Writes Althusser: "The economic cannot have the qualities of a *given* (of the immediately visible and observable, etc.) because its identification requires the concept of the structure of the economic, which in turn requires the concept of the structure of the mode of production, ... because its identification, therefore, presupposes the construction of its concept. The concept of the economic must be constructed *for each mode of production*" (R.C.: 183, in E.P. Thompson: 338). About the relations of production, Althusser says that "since these are 'relations', they cannot be thought Within the category subject". (op.cit.: 339). One would notice, the classic repetition of the functionalist separation of the social categories from social experience leading to kind of categorical stasis. This also amounts to arbitrary separation of a mode of production from the concrete historical processes, from its subject in concrete space and time. Even the dynamic component of Marxist methodology, its notion of dialectic and social process are in the structuralist metamorphosis rendered lifeless and limp. "Classes are", to Althusser, "functions of the process of production as a whole. They are not its subject, on the contrary, they are determined by its form" (R.C.: 267).

Thus, the "subject (or agent) of history disappears once again. Process, for the time, is reified. And since classes are "functions of production" (a process into which, it seems, no human agency could possibly enter), the way is thrown open once again deducing classes, class fractions, class ideologies ("true" and "false") from their imaginary positioning ... within a mode of production ... and this mode of production is conceived of as something other than its eventuation in historical process, and within" the ensemble of social relations", although in fact it exists only as a construction within a metaphysical oration" (E.P. Thompson: 1979). Both the notions of dialectic and social process in Marxist-structuralism appear as reincarnations of Hegelian epistemology.

It would thus appear that functionalism, structuralism and structuralist-Marxism, in their contemporary manifestations of epistemology and theory are faced with a crisis which they share in common. It is a crisis of concept formation which may be commensurate with the rules of validation and verification or which may be able to integrate the logical with the phenomenological, biographical with historical and theory with practice. The tensions in most efforts towards theorising in the recent past have pulled into two opposite directions: the ambition to explain and generalise nomologically has led to epistemological transcedentalism whereas the urge to validate and confirm empirically into an opposite and equally fruitless direction, of cognitive solipsism. In the search for a middle ground, between extreme formalism on the one hand, and raw empiricism on the other, many sociologists have proposed replacement, of the term 'concept' itself by mere workable operational categories which are general enough to enable comparison and specific enough simultaneously, to retain links with history constitutive of human experiences, social processes, their unfoldment and transformation. Peter Woorseley suggests that such terms may be called 'parameters' rather than concepts. Sartre on the other hand, commenting upon Althusser's treatment of social structure, suggests replacement of the term 'concept' by notion. He writes:

"Althusser, like Foucault, sticks to the analysis of structure. From the epistemological point of view, that amounts to returning to siding with the concept against *notion*. The concept is atemporal. One can study how concepts ate engendered one after the other within determined categories. But neither time itself nor, consequently, history; can be made the object of a concept. There is a contradiction in terms. When you introduce temporality, you come to see that within a temporal development the concept modifies itself. *Notion*, on the contrary, can be defined as the synthetic effort to produce an idea which develops itself by contradiction and its successive overcoming, and therefore, is homogeneous to development of things" (quoted in E.P. Thompson: 302, 1979). It is obvious that the concept of social structure may be better understood and operationalised for study if we treat it as a notion or study it through historico-social parameters rather than as formal category. It is better to treat it as a process, in a state of becoming rather than being, which leads to the fallacies of reification.

The symptoms of crisis in concepts and theories of social structure today also coincide with tendencies towards theoretical convergence. This has resulted more from the usage of theory in the understanding of social reality rather than from its logical or formal refinement. In other words, it is the process of operationalisation of theory which reveals the inadequacy of too narrow a formulation of the problem based upon the supposed premises of an individual theory. An interesting confirmation of this trend has been revealed in a survey conducted by the Research Committee on Economy and Society of the International Sociological Association during 1980. Three hundred questionnaires were sent out to social scientists in United States, Canada, Western Europe and Latin America. About one hundred who responded to the questionnaire on the item relating to the "present approaches and those on the horizon", believe that certain schools or offshoots of Marxism offer the most promise. One American sociologist studying power and the state, sees the Gramcian understanding of hegemony and crisis as the most promising for understanding the capitalist crisis. Another American feels that Karl Polanyi focussed our attention on the totality, both across-time and internationally as the pre-requisite for analysing any particular relationship between the economy and society—and was critical fore-runner for much of the dependency literature including the later development of world system thinking of Wallerestein. And a Brazilian sociologist believes that critical theory developed by the Frankfurt School holds the most promise because it tries to reconcile a Marxist inheritance with other approaches. Similarly, an Italian sociologist believes that Jurgen Habermas' work is the most promising for understanding economy and society, since he has raised the question of "reproducibility" of the global system. And a French-Canadian sociologist aptly stated that unlike previous theoretical and methodological approaches, the Marxist approach will continue to generate numerous studies because it has within it a capacity to change and develop. Or, as a Latin American sociologist put it, this approach opens innovative possibilities in methodology and in the construction of theory and explanatory design. A few of our scholars thought, a Marxist, combined with a Weberian approach has grown in importance during the past 20 years and held great promise for future research. In this regard, a Latin American political scientist studying comparative process of democratisation remarked that there has emerged 'a combination of a sophisticated neo-Marxism and neo-Weberian approach a la 'Economy and Society' combined with historical analysis. For him, the detailed study of changing social-economic (and state's) structures along an explicit historical dimension was by far the best way to look at phenomena which only exist as sets of constitutive inter-relationships and unfold along time (not as something that is first, say, economic and then afterwards combined with, say, social). Several scholars held Marxist functionalism as an approach to the study of economy and society. A Japanese sociologist thought, the most promising approach is synthetic blend of Marxism with functionalism for the analysis of structure of industrial society (see Makler *et.al;* in Bottomore *et.al:* 1982).

The crisis of convergence in sociological theory is also symptomatic. It calls for a movement away from mere formal logic of categories of system and social structure to their operationalisation as social and historical processes. This approach to the understanding of social structure evolves from sociological practice. "As sociology becomes more operational in its orientation and less formal, as the historical and symbolic nature of the social reality impinges more and more sharply upon sociologists's attempt to understand social reality, the focus I shifts from system-constructs to social processes. All system-constructs which look at society as conceptual typologies, such as feudal capitalist and socialist, or urban and rural, or modern or traditional, tend to become formal and abstract; abstraction is indeed necessary for any understanding of meaning and social structure but merely as a heuristic device. The formal system-constructs, however, use typologies which do not always function as heuristic devices that are candidates for empirical confirmation, but as ideological canopy for legitimation of a particular value judgement on social systems. Consequently, most such studies suffer from fallacy of affirmation, or create a situation where one set of system-indicators are at perpetual war with another set (feudalism-capitalism, semi-feudalism, pre-capitalism, etc.).

The operational sociology which is deeply grounded into the study of the concrete and the historical social reality, begins from the observation of processes. A systems notion is then arrived at from the character of the observed processes by a flexible application of analytical devices of all such 'theoretical paradigms' as may be relevant. It is this kind of sociological craftsmanship which does not feel satisfied with one particular 'theory', but wants to draw from a mix of them in an integrative perspective" (Singh, Yogendra: 1984: II).

A Scientific Approach

Within the field of theoretic convergence, Marxism offers the scientific approach for the study of social structure as social process. It is not to deny that Marxism at the hands of Althusser and many other structuralists, has preached to the contrary a dogma of formalism and neo-Hegelianism. This we have to guard against and follow the essential dialectic of the. Marxist method. The basic operational categories of this method are 'mode of production', 'social formation, class dialectic and historical, revolutionary transformation and change; The term 'mode of production' has been often vulgarised as economism on the one hand, and determinism on the other, causing much confusion in wider applicability of this concept. As Godelier rightly observes: "A mode of production is a reality which 'does not reveal itself' directly in any spontaneous and intimate experience of these agents who reproduce it by their activity ('indigenous' practices and representations), nor in any enquiries in the field or the knowledgeable external observations of professional anthropologists. A mode of production is a reality which requires to be reconstructed, to be reproduced in thought, in the very process of scientific knowledge. A reality exists as 'scientific fact' only when it is reconstructed within the field of scientific theory and its corresponding application.

This conclusion follows modern practice in the natural science (page 24, op. cit). Godelier further adds: "the most common error, among Marxists, is to confuse the study of the production process in a society with that of the labour processes, and to invest as many modes of production as there are labour processes.... A production process, in fact; consists not only of one or more labour process (man's relationship to man on the material level in a determined environment on the basis of a determined technology) but man's relationship to man, producers and non-producers, in the appropriation and control of the means of production (land, tools, raw materials, manpower) and the products of labour (hunting, grazing, gathering, fishing, agriculture, breeding, planting, handicrafts, etc.). These relations of production may be presented in the shape of kinship relations or relations of political or religious subordination, and the reproduction of the relations of production will then proceed through the reproduction of these kinship relations, or political or ideological subordination" (Godelier: 24-25).

Labour process, thus, in a wider historical meaning defines social structure through mode of production. Social formations are the building blocks of institutional foci that emerge through the functioning of different modes of production. The class structure is a concrete manifestation of the processes through which relations of production are historically patterned. It may imply a certain level and quality of labour process and its appropriation, but as a process and not as structure; class relations may take several forms quite atypical of a more general conceptual formulation. Instead of being differentiated and crystallised as the text-book theory of class states, class as a social process might inhere attributes that are structurally associated with other social formations, such as caste, ethnicity, estate, etc., in a de-differentiation mode of existence. It is, therefore, sociologically sounder to locate the reality of class in its process, in its historical becoming rather than in its structure and being. E.P. Thompson captures this idea when he states: "By class I understand a historical phenomenon, unifying a number of disparate and seemingly unconnected events, both in the raw material of experience and in consciousness. I emphasise that it is a historical phenomenon, I do not see class as a 'structure', nor even as a 'category', but as something which in fact happens (and can be shown to have happened) in human relationships ... More than this, the notion of class entails the notion of historical relationship. Like any other relationship, it is a fluency which evades analysis if we attempt to stop it dead at any given moment and anatomise its structure. The finest meshed sociological net cannot give as a pure specimen of class, any more than it can give us of deference or love" (Thompson E.P.: 11968: 8). Moreover, Thompson says: "There is today an ever-present temptation to suppose that class is a thing. This was not Marx's meaning, in his own historical writing, yet the error vitiates much later day 'Marxist' writing" (op.cit.: 1968:9).

Once we take a processual view of class and other social entities in the social structure, the understanding of change, both revolutionary and non-revolutionary ones becomes easy to comprehend. Such changes have to be seen in the context of history and social consciousness of the people concerned. Class consciousness is the way that human experiences in production relationship are articulated in cultural terms, in terms of economic and political interests, and the manner in which these lead to mobilisation for collective endeavours. The contradictions which lie at the base of the class relations, and give it a revolutionary potential, in the multiplex of production relations take not necessarily a dualistic form of polarisation as widely postulated, but operate in a pluralistic intersection of relationships. Once we shed economism from the notion of mode of production and production relationship, these class engendered mobilisations might not only be grounded in economic but also political, religious, cultural, ,kinship and other forms of articulation of interests. The relationship between infra-structure and super-structure in this frame of thinking takes on a historical and dynamic form.

Indian Experience

Conceptually speaking, sociologists and social anthropologists in India for several decades analysed social structure with the help of caste, class, occupation, etc., not as processes but as things. Durkheimean fallacy of functional positivism via Radcliffe Brown influenced a whole generation of older sociologists. A model of caste or class was for such analysis assumed in the abstract. The varna model, the notions of pollution and purity and hierarchy were such boxes through which the Indian social structure was characterised. Louis Dumont's structuralist contribution on caste and social structure in India in his Homo Hierarchicus epitomises this approach. In all such treatments, the emphasis on the historical, the total or on the linkages was by-passed, and the elements which typified were selectively exaggerated. Hence, one would notice in most such studies of social structure in India a pathetic neglect of macro-structural treatment, of interaction between caste and class and economy and polity or on the role of state in production of social structure. There were a few exceptions, however, as R.K. Mukherjee's study of dynamics in rural Bengal, C.S. Ghurye's treatment of the tribes, caste and occupation. D.P. Mukherji and Radha Kamal Mukherjee could also be seen emphasising the historical and comparative perspective. There could be a few others as well. But the dominant tendency in the mainstream of Indian Sociology of the 1950's and 1960's was that of functionalist formalism, which we have criticised. Only a few studies used historical or Marxist perspective. Those using Marxist method did not use the refinement of the mode of production approach in a truly dialectical sense. The historical sociology too was confined to the study of subsystems.

The 1970's and 1980's in the Indian sociology exemplify a departure from the earlier approaches. Social structure now was studied from a more comparative and dynamic (though not dialectical) perspective, at least analytically. Instead of studying caste or class as things or as reified categories, or as models, the perspective shifted on parameters. Some important parameters that were used were those of status, wealth and power. Social structure, its dynamics and change was observed by the degree to which the overlap or summation of all the three principles in determining the place of individuals or groups in social position was effective or otherwise. Differentiation or independent functioning of the three parameters in defining the position meant change and dissonance in social structure. The limitation of this approach was caused once again by its formalism. The notions of status, wealth and power were treated analytically as equivalents of the principles of caste, class and polity, the traditional social structural categories, and this analogous mode of thinking led to little intensive study of the internal composition and processes within these three categories themselves. Hence, the thesis of open and closed social structure (with overlap of parameters or without) or principle of stratification was largely devoid of a sense of history and dialectic of experiences, collective or individual. It made some advance over former stasis of categories but found itself a victim of analytical formalism.

In the uses of the terms class and caste for the study of social structure in India, Suraj Bandopadhyay finds that most studies use the term class only as a label, without recognition of interlinkages. He concludes that "the domain where such an analytical scheme may surely contribute effectively will be related to gaining a conceptual clarity in understanding the implicit process linking caste and class systems: whereas two mutually exclusive conceptualisations of the system, or as basically separate but sometimes overlapping components of a plural society, are as different lines in substantively the same mosaic" (1977: 131). This emphasis on process and the dynamics of interlinkages is an emerging focus in the study of social structure in India.

The 1970's and 1980's, also witnessed the rise of Marxist and marxological studies of the aspects of Indian social structure using the mode of production approach. Kathlein Gough in the area of kinship, Joan Mencher in the analysis of social mobility and stratification, Lindberg and Jurfield in rural sociology are some of the studies which use the logic and method of Marxism in various degrees. Mode of production is variously described by these sociologists as either feudalism-capitalism or as semi-feudalistic or pre-capitalistic. In each case, the social structure in question is deductively portrayed from a pure typology of mode of production. This is particularly so in the study of kinship by Kathlein Gough. Sometimes, Indian social structure and its processes are analysed taking the arrival of the capitalistic mode of production in India for granted, or at least as being the pre-dominant form. I.P. Desai, in his otherwise meticulous analysis of the occupational mobility and social change in India, bases most of his premises on the assumption that capitalism in the rational form of monetization has already replaced feudalism in India. Others find Indian social structure still being entrenched in feudalism or feudalistic mode of production relationships. If one takes a micro-structural view, all such observations can be proved right. From a comparative macro-perspective, however, most such observations or premises though right in limited fields, do not add up to a general perspective or theory. The major limitation in such approaches to studying social structure, is the assumption of a system-state as a theoretic model for observation of the social processes. The approach should on the contrary be reverse, building system state models from the historical and experiential data of social processes (see, Singh Y: 1972: 137-38 in Srinivas et. al. 1972). The fault does not lie in the concepts of feudalism, capitalism or other modes of production postuated, but in the methodology of their confirmation or disconfirmation.

There is a new tendency, however, to recognise this and look at social structure from a historical perspective and as social process. This has resulted from wider affirmation of a dynamic and dialectical rather than deterministic notion of mode of production, and the tendency to construct the notion of social structure from observed historical experiences in social and cultural settings. In the studies of caste or class the emphasis has shifted from dichotomy to dialectical interlinkages, which bring out the role of these structural entities as social processes. I.P. Desai in a recent analysis of whether caste could be the basis for definition of backwardness or not, has applied a processual view on caste, class and occupation. He writes: The situation is quite different from what it was 25 years ago. David Pocock used to say in private conversation that in inter-caste marriages in the past, the individual did not reject the caste, but the casts rejected him. Now not only caste does not reject him but accepts him. The individuals of the caste use him for their individual secular interests. The growth of these secular interests feeds the interest conscious unities which operate in economic, political and social fields. Let it not be understood that caste endogamy has ceased to exist. It will continue for quite some time. But its sanctions are not and will not be group sanctions of a caste. It will largely be due to individual circumstances and the convenience of the group will simply aquiese in it. Thus, caste divisiveness is giving place to divisiveness on a secular basis (I.P. Desai:

1984, page: 112). A.M. Shah supports the evidence of cleavages in the principle of hierarchy in the caste system resulting from occupational and economic divisions. The divisions also exist and diversify on rural-urban differentiation.

The processes operating in the social structure of India today offer evidence of fluidity in the notions of caste and class. We observed in our study of rural class and caste structure in the eastern U.P. villages the evidence of this process as far back as mid-1960's. The relationship between ideology, culture, economy, social forces and political organisation or mobilisation with the structure of caste-class fluidity marks a new process of re-structuration in the Indian social structure. Dipankar Gupta rightly observes: "It is the structuration that ideological or super-structural elements get a semantic content and meaning. This structuration makes sense because of the selective manner in which certain elements are given salience to provide a charter for class action. At another point different aspects of these non-univocal elements can be activated, or wholly new element may be brought in (Dipankar Gupta: 1983, page 20: 1993)." We had observed how on issues relating to economic and political interests a set of castes vertically hierarchised culturally, would throw up a class front, a class mobilisation with political support, and also succeed in fighting the class battle. Once, the class issues became secondary after their realisation or otherwise the process of class is submerged in other sociological divides of occupation, caste, kinship and communities. This holds true for caste mobilisation as well, which has shown in India wide-spread evidence of cleavages and associations both on horizontal and vertical lines. As the forces of social and economic change gain ground and expand, new social cleavages and formations are continually in the making. The notions of feudalism, capitalism or those of caste and class would have to be carefully scrutinised in India for their successful operationalisation and relevance.

To sum up: Concepts for understanding social structure in sociology have suffered generally either from nominalism or formalism. The trend towards nominalism resulted from observation of structures (a great strength of sociology in the beginning) without emphasis on comparison or generalisation. Formalism in concepts, on the contrary, had its origin in the reverse direction, the enthusiasm for over-generalisation, without anchorage in history and specificity. These errors have pervaded in almost all varieties of theoretic orientations, functionalist, structuralist and Marxist. Its realisation today, therefore, has contributed to a movement towards conceptual and theoretical integration or even convergence. It has also led to new emphasis in the study of social structures as processes rather than forms, on history and culture than on timeless abstractions. To study social structure as a process one would be well advised to draw from several theoretic insights, but Marxist notion of mode of production, social formation and social praxis offer maximum advantages, provided these notions are used dialectically with a sense of history and specificity, provided also that the notion of mode of production is not reified in typological forms but left open to operailonalisation in the contexts of social and historical experiences of various societies. This orientation in the study of social structure is also more viable as among most sociological theories, Marxism to the maximum extent offers the advantages of observing the dialectic of interaction between state power and society, between infrastructure and super-structure of social formations, that state and its political economy generates as forces for changes, in the social structure. In India, state has played a very crucial role in setting into motion social forces which have positively and negatively characterised the process of change or otherwise in the social structure. Both functionalism and structuralism, lag far behind in their conceptual structure to take cognisance of this reality in the understanding of social structure, although in the areas of ideology, culture, kinship and family their contribution is more pervasive and lasting. It would be better if Indian sociologists selectively combined the advantages that functionalist and structuralist perspectives offer with those notions they find advantageous from Marxist categories. At the level of meta-theory and epistemology, however, not functionalism or structuralism but creative dialectics offers a more solid ground.

REFERENCES

Godelier M. *Perspectives in Marxist Anthropology,* London, Cambridge University Press, 1978.

Dipankar Gupta, "Sociologism, Marxism and the Anthropological Imagination," *Journal of Contemporary Asia,* Vol. 13, No.1., 1983.

Desai, J.P. "Should 'Caste' be the Basis for Recognising Backwardness?" *Economic and Political Weekly,* Vol. XIX, No. 28, July 14,1984.

Makler Harry et.al. "Recent Trends in Theory and Methodology," (ed.) *Sociology: The State Of Art,* ISA, 1982.

Suraj Bandopadhyay. "Caste 'Lost' and Caste 'Regained': Some Aspects of a Sociology of Empirical Research on Village India," in M.N. Srinivas et.al. (eds.) *Dimensions of Social Change in India,* New Delhi: Allied Publishers, 1977.

Singh Yogendra. "The Changing Patterns of Social Stratification in India," in M.N. Srinivas et.al. (eds.) *Dimensions of Social Change in India,* Allied Publishers, 1977.

"Relevant Sociology (I)" *Relevant Sociology: A Journal of Contemporary Sociology,* Vol. I., No.1, 1984.

Thompson, E.P. *The Poverty of Theory and Other Essays,* London: Marlin Press; 1979.

_____ *The Making of the English Working Class,* London: Penguin Press, 1968.

Chapter 12

Social Stratification

During the past four decades, sociology of stratification has made rapid strides in India. No other area of concern has perhaps occupied attention of sociologists as much as this problem. Its orientation has been shaped by our social and historical legacy, ideology of the nation-state and the quest to establish a socialist society based on the principles of equality, justice, secularism and democracy. It has also been influenced by the continuing historical interest in the studies of caste, tribe, and oppressed communities initiated by the British administrator-cum-social anthropologists and its continuity and change in the studies by the Indian sociologists and social anthropologists. The focus upon establishing a casteless and classless society in the national movement led by Gandhiji and his emphasis upon the liberation of the 'Harijans' and socially oppressed communities in India, added momentum to the wider interest in sociology of stratification. Most studies during the 1930's to 1950's in these areas, however, studied caste, tribe and communities as individual sub-systems, postulating a degree of social and economic autonomy for them which indeed they did not enjoy. The structure and functions of systems and subsystems of caste and tribes were profiled in detail but the linkages of these systems with other institutions in the wider Indian society such as its political economy and administration, etc. were either neglected or were treated marginally. Nevertheless, these studies made substantial contributions in establishing a scientific foundation for Indian social stratification studies later, in terms of methodology, conceptual schemes and generation of data for comparison and analysis.

After India gained Independence, studies in social stratification formed part of most empirical studies of villages, town and urban centres, the areas in which most sociologists engaged themselves during this period. The relationships between caste and tribe and caste and community were explored by a few sociologists mostly in search of conceptual clarification. Among the important features of these studies were: focus upon ritual bases of caste stratification, structural-functional perspective in analysis, collection of data through fieldwork observation and limited space-time boundary in delineation of the system of caste stratification. With few exceptions, studies of social stratification neglected the use of historical sources of data, did not go into the questions of origin or evolution and did not attempt to view caste system in the macro-structural perspective of social transformation. Most studies tended to be diagnostic or descriptive with a micro-cosmic view of social reality. The emphasis was on mapping out the social terrain in India, rather than raising issues of concepts, ideology or methods. Class analysis as a frame of reference was either absent or negligible in most studies of social stratification. Most studies at this stage of Indian sociology focused upon caste, tribe and village community from a descriptive perspective. The analytical notion of social stratification was present in these studies only as an inferential aspects of the empirical observations.

By the 1960's, however, the conceptual and methodological issues became basic in the studies of social stratification in India. An important development in this direction was the shift in emphasis from observation of empirical entities of social stratification, pre-eminent in most studies of the 1950's to the *principles* of relationship among these entities of stratification. In the study of caste stratification, Louis Dumont's contribution would stand out as the most significant one. He raised the level of studies of social stratification much above the substantivist plane to that of questions of theory and ideology. In his sociology, both tend to be integral parts of one another. This trend was supplemented by, though from a different direction, the increasing number of studies of social stratification using Marxist theory and method. Here, the class frame of historical materialist analysis was applied. These studies, though still fewer in sociology, came largely from the economists studying the agrarian social structure of India. Moreover, many systematic studies of social stratification using analytical conceptual frame were conducted. Andre Beteille's use of the conceptual categories of 'caste', 'class' and 'power' for the analysis of social stratification in a South Indian village illustrates the shift towards 'principles' and theory. F.G. Bailey in his theoretical essays and empirical studies of the tribe-caste-nation linkages in Orissa also amplifies this trend. Both Beteille and Bailey have used the notions of 'open and closed' social stratification in their treatment of this process.

These developments in the social stratification studies had several general consequences for sociology in India. First, sociological studies entered a new level of maturity in respect of theory. The debates now ranged about choices among conceptual typologies versus continua, historical specificity versus comparison, structure-function versus conflict and dialectics versus ideology in the analytical propositions of social stratification. Secondly, social stratification studies now increasingly tended to be problem oriented both conceptually and substantively. This is reflected in two directions: first, more and more studies began to focus upon problems of caste and class exploitation, economic, political and cultural domination I and the relationship between poverty, social and cultural alienation and distributive justice. The studies of the scheduled castes and tribes, of backward classes and the dominant castes or communities formed a large proportion where the analytical approach was that of social stratification. Moreover, studies of social stratification developed an independent theoretical focus instead of being a marginal element in the study of a village, township or community. In such studies several theoretical tendencies emerged, such as structuralism, structural-functionalism, systemic theory, structural historicism and Marxism. On closer examination of these studies, it would, however, be revealed that most theoretical tendencies have a degree of overlap or paradigm mixes. This accords well with universal tendency in sociological theory during this period, as also with the proposition that a general theory in sociology remains problematic. It is probably with this view in mind that one talks of 'quasi' or 'atheoretic theory' in social sciences and sociology. This indicates the ambiguous and complex position of theory in sociology of social stratification.

The difficulties of theorising in the domain of social stratification are linked with the very fundamental philosophical issues that are involved. Sociologists have raised these issues in the context of the nature of equality and inequality among men. Others have linked it with the problem of social order. The notion of social order offers a meeting point both for dealing with the problems of so called 'natural inequality' and its social expression either in the principles of moral voluntarism or social contract. The theory of social stratification is thus organically linked with the theory of social order. The questions related to these issues have been recurrently raised in the Indian sociology. The discussions on the nature of caste and class in Indian society have led sociologists to the perspective on Indian tradition, its moral order and its functional or utilitarian significance. Curiously, whenever the focus in the study of caste in India has shifted on tradition, the historical or even speculative questions of its origin and comparison with similar institutions elsewhere have also arisen. With the dominance of the functionalist orientation, however, the quest for the history and origin of caste-class receded in the background. The theoretical questions related to the principles of social stratification in Indian society have vacillated in accordance with the relative role and influence of either of these two tendencies.

The emerging conceptual and theoretical concerns in studies of social stratification have culminated into several new orientations during the 1970's and 1980's. Some of these that have greater significance are: (1) debate on the role of ideology in the paradigms of social stratification, (2) revial of historical and evolutionary perspectives, (3) emergence of dialectical paradigm as a new theoretical orientation in social stratification studies, and finally (4) increasing concern about issues of relevance both from social and conceptual points of view in the studies of social stratification. These developments have resulted from the changing nature of theoretical and methodological orientations of sociology at the global level and also from the changes within the cognitive structure of Indian sociology. Its inner dialectic, its changing professional character and social concerns have also contributed to these developments.

Ideology and Social Stratification

The issue of ideology in the studies of social stratification has emerged during this period in two main contexts: first, as a general theoretical problem of sociological method, and secondly, as a problem of social determination of concepts and themes of studies of social stratification. In the first context, both structuralism and Marxism as theoretical paradigms for social stratification studies in India have incorporated the notion of ideology. It forms an organic elements of theorising. Louis Dumont in his well known study of the caste system as 'hierarchy' assigns ideology an important place as a component of the structuralist paradigm. The term ideology in his analysis has the connotation of ideas and norms derived from the Hindu civilization of which the caste system is an archtypical manifestation. The dominant principle in its normative structure is that of 'hierarchy' contained in the dialectical relationship between the principles of purity and pollution in the ritual and behavioural domains of the system. The central issue in the study of social stratification according to Louis Dumount is thus, the ideology of the caste system and its significance to the comparative study of social structure.

The notion of ideology despite having a key role in the Marxist theory of social structure and stratification has been found to be unevenly emphasised in the Indian studies of social stratification. In Karl Marx's own writings, ideology is treated as an organic element in all cognitive processes. It is reflected in the mystification between 'form' and 'substance'. His notions of fetishism of commodities", 'alienation of labour', and his distinction between 'infrastructure and superstructure' are examples of the significance of ideology in the formation of concepts and propositions in sociological studies. The task of social scientists according to Marx rests in the de-mystification of the fallacies in the choice of sociological categories and methods in establishing a proper relationship of these with social praxis and relevance. Marx's own formulation refers to the dual level of ideological mooring of knowledge, first, in the mystification of sociological categories for the study of social reality, and secondly, obfuscation of social praxis due to a specific class character of the production of knowledge.

The Marxist studies of the Indian social stratification raise these ideological issues but not in a comprehensive manner, Most studies focus upon the class. background of sociologists as being the key determinant of the place of ideology in their work. A distinction between the 'bourgeois', and the 'Marxist' sociologists is often made for ideological debunking of the non-Marxist studies of social stratification without, however, seriously questioning the cognitive or theoretical framework of such studies, especially as Marx envisaged. In the process, pertinent gaps are often identified without, however, successfully refuting the paradigm as a whole. A more creative aspect of the Marxist studies of social stratification is the 'mode of production' approach on which much empirical data have been recently generated. The manner of its operationalisation largely by the economists and historians is such that the notion of ideology plays a relatively marginal role in its formulation. The focus is more upon empirical indicators rather than upon normative presuppositions behind those indicators as such, except in a more generalised form. The pre-eminent role of ideology as reflected in the Marxist studies of social stratification is to establish its class character as such. It deals with ideology only at the social level of its manifestation and leaves out of purview the deeper aspect of its existence in the cognitive structure of sociological categories.

A related development in the assessment of the role of ideology in the studies of social stratification which in some cases bears relationship also with the Marxist tradition, is the emergence of 'counter-Brahamanical ideology' of the caste system in India. This ideology, largely reinforced by the increasing mobilization of the protest movements and the rise in the social consciousness of the educated classes among the deprived communities, tribes, scheduled castes and backward classes, questions the validity of the ritual model of the Hindu caste system based as it is on the worldview of pollution and purity. It attempts to re-interpret several myths and legends of the Hindu and Budhistic traditions to explain how the class and power domination of the 'twice-born' castes established the Brahamanical ideology of the caste into a position of unchallenged supremacy from among the two competing ideologies of social structure in India. One, based on the Brahamanical model of caste and the other, on a caste-less model of groups and communities based on occupational specialization. The latter is reflected though in an implicit form in the Budhist literature and tradition. The Brahamanical model, however, prevailed in the competition for power, which is symbolised according to the proponents of the counter-Brahamanical ideology in the myth of Bali (king), who was condemned to exile in the netherworld for challenging the supremacy of the Braharnanical worldview as it were.

This counter-Brahamanical ideology of caste finds reinforcement through the conversion of a large number of the Harijans and other scheduled caste in India to Buddhism in several parts of the country. It forms an important part of the ideology of the *Dalit* movement and its agenda for social reform and protest. There are a few examples also in the mainstream of sociological writings where ideological interpretations of the contributions of fellow sociologists has been alluding to their caste origin. A perspective in sociology has grown according to which the social and class origin of sociologists is held accountable for a good deal of biases in the choice of themes, concepts, methods and generalisations on social problems. Specially, while studying the problems of the exploited and weaker sections of society, several sociologists both Indian and Western have held that a more objective perspective would emerge if the reality is observed empathically through the eyes of the victims themselves. This supposedly involves beyond empathy greater involvement of sociologists coming from the weaker sections for such studies to correct the imbalance.

The emergence of this consciousness during the 1960's, became stronger by 1970's and 1980's. It got further impetus as the process of educational and social mobility among the weaker sections increased; the implementation of public policy of the state over the past decades has resulted in the emergence of an articulate intelligentia among these groups which can indeed give a practical shape to this requirement. The ideological debate relates to the significance of caste in the Indian social structure and tradition and the choice of relevant social policies for adequate response to bring about social transformation in the Indian society in accordance with the objectives of social justice, freedom and equality as laid down in the Constitution. As ideologies often constitute the axiomatic domain of the normative structure, it is difficult to enter into questions of their objectivity or otherwise. But the very emergence of this counter-Braharnanical ideology of caste and social stratification marks a new phase of development in the conceptual and menthodological perspective on studies of this problem in sociology.

Evolutionary Perspective

Another noteworthy trend which seems to have revived during the 1970's onwards in the study of social stratification is the revival of the themes of origin or evolution of the institutions of caste, occupational groups and classes in India. An associated new phenomenon in this development is the increasing use of history and historiography in the analysis of social institutions in India. The three factors that seem to explain this trend are: (1) the decline in functional paradigm of social stratification, which took a completely a-historical view of institutions and structures of society, (2) the rise in the dialectical and historical materialist paradigm of social analysis with the revival of Marxism in social sciences after mid-1960's and (3) the greater ideologization of the sociology of social stratification through the emerging new consciousness of the mobile classes from among the weaker sections of society. All these factors have largely converged together in the realm of Indian social sciences in general and in sociology in particular during the 1970-1980 period.

One set of studies have re-opened the question of origin of caste in India by attempting to explain its origin in ecological and occupational differentiation of groups into hereditary entities over a period of time. Others attempt to seek its genesis in the structure of domination, especially cultural domination of a set of communities over others on the basis of superior exploitation of wealth and power. The studies using Marxist methods which-increased substantially during the 1970's and 1980's have brought historical depth to bear upon the studies of caste-class relationship by attempting to sketch out its evolutionary path through the changing modes of production and production relationships. Very recently, a debate on the specific pattern of the caste mode of production has been postulated by some scholars. The outcome of these new orientations is not that a scientific thesis on the origin of caste stratification in India has been established, but its significance lies in the reflection of ideological tensions in the sociology of stratification, its theory and methods.

The pre-dominance of the functional method in the studies of caste and class relations and its patterns in India during the 1950's and 1960's had contributed to a rich harvest of field data, indepth observation of the structure and values of these institutions and their interlinkages with other social, economic and political institutions. But a major limitation of these studies was their static portrayal of the institutions, particularly caste and occupational structure of rural and urban society. In the functional postulates being also founded upon a consensus ideology of normative voluntarism, the reality of social stratification was viewed in most such studies from the perspective of social stability and continuity rather than conflict and change. The notion of change of necessity brings in the idea of time, history and dialectics. These elements of sociological analysis were missing from most early studies of social stratification. Also most such studies were based mainly upon empirical observations of social stratification in the setting of a village, or a town, and these did not make use of historical records nor did they use a comparative macro-social perspective.

The limitations of the functionalist model became increasingly obvious to sociologists in India during the 1970's and 1980's as elements of social conflict and dissensus arising from social inequalities of wealth and power began to come to surface as the results of planned development, and social transformation began to show results. The new developments in social sciences, particularly history, economics, political science, psychology and behavioural sciences also reinforced this process. Historians increasingly looked at social structure and its formations in India in a broad historical time frame; some schools in historiography, particularly the subaltern approach to history even undertook explorations of substructures and subcultures of society in depth both in term of time and space. The influence of Marxist orientation in the formulation of conceptual schemes and methods of social analysis among economists, particularly agricultural economists threw up new insights into the processes of social stratification in rural India. Their findings influenced the sociological paradigms of stratification studies. Similar trends were also visible in other social sciences. All this added up to the emergence of a historical and evolutionary framework in the studies of social stratification.

Dialectical Orientation

The emphasis on history and questions of origin led social stratification studies into the direction of new methodological awareness. An important development in this regard is the emergence of the dialectical orientation. This took two main operational forms in Indian sociology: first, an emphasis on the observation of social processes of social stratification and its emergent properties rather than substance or form. Secondly, the shift in focus from the consensus ideology of social stratification to the ideology of social dialectics, conflict and dissensus. In studies using Marxist theory these became the basic parameters of observation and analysis. The focus on social processes arises from a debate on the methodology of operationalising the notion of social stratification. Should the reality of caste or class be sought in the substantive properties of these social entities or in their processes of formation? It is argued that emphasis on substantive properties of the parameters of stratification, such as caste and class have contributed to a static and a-historical perspective in studies. Assuming social entities to exist as *being* and not as *becoming*, has some logical consequences for the interpretation of data and uses of the notions of social transformation.

These consequences in the field of social stratification are manifest both in Marxist and non-Marxist studies. We have already mentioned about the partiality in comprehension of the processes of social stratification in studies using the functional frame of reference. The focus so predominant in this method was to portray the reality of social stratification as a question of maintaining social order rather than its transformation. Many studies have recognised how the significance of these entities rest today in the extent to which these contribute to or hinder the processes of social mobility and restructuration of positions in terms of wealth, status and power. Too much emphasis on their 'being', as evident in not only functionalist but also structuralist studies, results into abstraction of social reality from its historical dialectics. In empirical sense, the question related to these issues have arisen in the analysis of caste and class in India. Traditionally, these institutions were studied either through a set of attributes (indicators) .or through a set of interactional patterns related to social, economic and cultural dealings. In both these approaches emphasis rested upon the facticity of caste-class phenomenon, its structure or set of relationships and their quality. In the Marxist studies the structural reality of caste and class is seen through modes of production defined in terms of system-states such as 'feudalism' or 'capitalism'. Intensive studies have, however, revealed that both caste and class situations and their patterns of relationship not only converge but these also operate in transient or even interchanging forms of relationships which are not easy to dichotomise as social processes. Undoubtedly, caste does offer a more enduring set of relationships that constitute the social, economic, political and cultural forces generated in the larger society. Hence, what is of interest in the studies of caste or class in India today is not only their form as social institutions per se, but the nature of their dynamics, the degree of caste-ness in caste or 'class-ness' in the class. structure. This has been widely identified by several sociologists studying caste and class relationships and its changes in the contemporary Indian society. Novelty of this approach has contributed to a debate in the Marxist, structuralist as well as the functionalist circles of sociology and social sciences. Among the historians' the contributions made by the subaltern approach to historiography has added to this awareness. It not only links the social processes of the macro-structures with micro-structures but also the notion of social order with social processes as such.

These developments have led on the one hand, to further intensification of cognitive and methodological contexts of sociological paradigms such as structuralism, ethnomethodology, ethnosociology, Marxism, and functionalism, etc.; on the other, an increasing degree of theoretical convergence has also taken place in the analysis and understanding of social reality in general and the process of social stratification in particular. This is evident first, from the wider social science approach to the studies of social stratification during the 1970's and 1980's which goes beyond the disciplinary confines of sociology or social anthropology. The historians, economists, political scientists and psychologists are making significant contributions today which have relevance for the understanding of social stratification. Secondly, with this inter-disciplinary orientation in the study of social stratification, there exists greater possibility of theoretical convergence. Indeed, there are indications that such a process, of theoretical convergence is taking place in the studies of social stratification. The subaltern historians show increasing evidence of a synthesis between the Marxist and structuralist paradigms for the analysis of class and social movements. Most recent studies of social stratification conducted from the Marxist theoretical frame show increasing concern with notions of tradition, structure and function along with that of dialectics and transformation. The functionalist studies of social stratification have shown acute concern with issues of conflict, contradiction and historical processes, The increasing interest in the studies of social movement and its linkages with caste and class relationships, the studies of agrarian, demographic and urban structures, the processes of political and economic formations and the study of ideology behind social stratification reflect these emerging tendencies. The overarching orientation in these studies is to focus upon social dialectics rather than social order.

Issues of Relevance

The question of social relevance has been existent in studies of social stratification in India since early times. The context of the debate on relevance, however, has been changing. In the 1950's, most studies were oriented to processes of social, economic, political and cultural developments under the inspiration of the national effort for planned social. transformation. Studies were focusing upon community development, panchayat processes, role of caste, class and elite formations in the development of rural, urban and industrial sectors of society. Some studies were indeed mainly sociographic but most were interested in studying social developments and in identifying institutions and practices which aided or inhibited such processes. The question of relevance was largely identified with question of planned development. In 1960's, there was a major change in the ideological outlook on the problem of relevance. Two directions in which this issue was debated were, the epistemological and the social context of relevance. The first direction led to the debate on the cognitive and theoretical nature of Indian sociology, in which the debate on social stratification figured as a question of comparison of caste and class. As Dumont argued, the distinction between the hierarchical principle of caste organisation in India from the equalitarian principle of class organisation in the European society evoked such interest in sociology. Similarly, the debate on the appropriateness or relevance of paradigms for the study of Indian social reality including social stratification emerged in this category of the questions of relevance. The second context of relevance was related to the contribution that social stratification studies could make accelerating social praxis and social change in India.

The concern with social praxis and change in the studies of social stratification has diversified its conceptual and operational orientations. In the process of social development, the significance of the principles of social stratification, such as caste and class inequalities have now been viewed more and more in terms of conflict and contradictions. The earlier focus upon non-critical acceptance of the policies of change has given way to critical analysis of both processes and policies of change and development to ensure social equality and justice in society. This has added much relevance to the theoretical approaches to the study of social stratification from the perspectives of critical theory and Marxism. The quest for understanding the basic principles and processes of structure and change in social stratification in the Indian society has also diversified during the 1970's and 1980's. The studies are not confined merely to the studies of caste and class. The process of modernization and restructuration in the Indian society that have been taking place for the past several decades has brought into focus many new issues of social stratification, such as the professions, elites, categories of weaker sections of society, women, children, tribes and scheduled castes, etc. winch constitute new domains of inequalities and equalities. Study of these social entities and their role in the process of social stratification in the context of modernization and development is the new direction that offers a new perspective on relevance. Sociology has yet to fully recognise the significance of these emergent social formations and structural entities influencing the principles and processes of social stratification in India. But the awareness in this direction has already begun taking root. This, along with other new orientations in the study of social stratification, offers new fruitful dimensions of growth in the Indian sociology.

References

Abercrombie N., Hill S. and Turner B.S., *The Penguin Dictionary of Sociology,* New York: Penguin Press, 1984.

Ames M.M., "Structural Dimensions of Family Life in the Steel City of Jamshedpur, India" in Singer Milton (ed) *Entrepreneurship and Modemisation of Occupational Cultures in South Asia,* Duke University Press, 1973.

Banaji J., "Chayanov, Kautsky, Lenin: Considerations Towards a Synthesis," *Economic and Political Weekly,* Vol. XI, No. 40, 1976.

Bandopadhyay Suraj, "Caste 'Lost' and Caste 'Regained': Some Aspects of a Sociology of Empirical Research on Village India" in Srinivas M.N. et, al (ed.) *Dimensions of Social Change in India,* New Delhi: Allied Publishers, 1977.

Baxi Upendra, *The Crises of the Indian Legal System,* New Delhi: Vikas Publishing House, 1982.

Bhalla Sheila, "Agricultural Growth: Role of Institutional and Infrastructural Factors," *Economic and Political Weekly,* Vol. XII, Nos. 45, 46, 1977.

Bose N.K., *Culture and Society in India,* New Delhi: India Publishing House, 1977.

Bouddieu Pierre, *Guardian Weekly,* February 2, 1992.

Chandra Bipan, *Nationalism and Colonialism in Modem India,* New Delhi: Orient Longman, 1981.

The Rise and Growth of Economic Nationalism in India, Delhi: People's Publishing House, 1966.

Chatterjee Parthta, *Nationalist thought and the Colonial World: A Derivative Discourse,* Delhi: Oxford University Press, 1986.

Cohen Allan, *Tradition, Change and Conflict in Indian Family Business,* Hague: Mouton, 1974.

Cohn B.S., "From Indian Status to British Contract" *Journal of Economic History,* 21-613-618, 1961.

Davis Kingsley, *Population of India and Pakistan,* New York: Free Press, 1958.

Desai A.R., *Social Background of Indian Nationalism,* Bombay: Oxford University Press, 1948.

Sociology of the Underprivileged, Inaugural Address, 5th U.P. Sociology Conference, Kanpur: University of Kanpur, 1983.

Desai. I.P., "Should 'Caste' be the Basis for Recognising Backwardness?", *Economic and Political Weekly,* Vol. XIX. No. 28, July 14, 1984.

Some aspects of Family in Mahuua: A Sociological Study of jointness in a small town, Bombay: Asia Publishing House, 1964.

The Craft of Sociology and Other Essays. Delhi: Ajanta Publications, 1981.

Dumont Louis, "Nationalism and Communalism," *Contributions to Indian Sociology,* Paris: Mouton and Co. ,1964.

Fox R.G., "Pariah Capitalism and Traditional Indian Merchants, Past and Present," in Singer M (ed) *op. cit.,* 1973.

Gadgil D.R., *Origin of the Modern Indian Business Class: An Interim Report,* New York: Institute of Pacific Relations, 1959.

Gallanter M., "The Aborted Restoration of Indigenous Law in India." *Comparative Studies in Society and History.* Vol. 14. No. I. 1972.

"The Displacement of Traditional Law in Modem India," *Journal of Social Issues,* Vol. 24, Nov. 4,1968.

Gandhi J.S., *Lawyers and Touts: A Study of the Sociology of the Legal Profession.* New Delhi: Hindustan Publishing Corporation, 1982.

Godelier M., *Perspectives in Marxist Anthropology.* London: Cambridge University Press. 1978.

Goode W.J., *World Revolution and Family Patterns,* New York: Free Press, 1963.

Gore M.S., *Urbanization. and Family Change,* Bombay: Popular Prakashan, 1968.

Guha Ranjit (ed), *Subaltern Studies* I. Delhi: Oxford University Press, 1982.

Gupta Dipankar, *Nativism in a Metropolis: Shiv Sena in Bombay,* New Delhi: Manohar, 1982.

"Sociologism, Marxism and Anthropological Imagination," *Journal of Contemporary Asia.* Vol. 13. No.1. 1983.

Haksar Nandita, "Justice for Common Man," *The Hindustan Times.* New Delhi: May 22. 1983.

Harry Makler et, al., "Recent Trends in Theory and Methodology," (ed) *Sociology: The State of Art,* ISA, 1982.

I.C.S.S.R, *Status of Women in India: A Synopsis of the Report of the National Committee,* New Delhi: Allied Publishers, 1975.

Iyre V.K. Krishna, "The Indian Constitution: Our Founding Deed and Our Fighting Creed-Some Thoughts on Their Future," First S.K. Sinha Memorial Lecture, New Delhi: 1982.

Kamenka D. and R. Tay Alic Erh-Soon, "Socialism, Anarchism and Law," *Law and Society: The Crisis in Legal Ideals* (ed) Robert Brown et. al; London: Edward Arnold, 1978.

Kane P.V., *Hindu Customs and Modern Law,* Bombay: Bombay University, 1950.

Khare R.S., "Indigenous Culture and Lawyer's Law in India," *Comparative Study in Society and History,* Vol. 14, No.1, 1972.

Kolenda P., *Regional Differences in Family Structure in India,* Jaipur: Rawat Publications, 1987.

Krishnaji N., "Agrarian Structure and Family Formation: A Tentative Hypothesis," *Economic and Political Weekly,* March, 1980.

Marriott M., "New Peasants in an Old Village," in Singer M.(ed) *op. cit.*

Mehta S.D., *The Indian Cotton textile Industry: An Economic Analysis,* Bombay: 1953.

Mines M., "Tamil Muslim Merchants in India's Industrial Development," in Singer M. (ed) *op. cit.*

Mitchell G.D., *A New Dictionary of Sociology,* London: Routledge & Kegan Paul, 1981.

Moore W.E., *Impact of Industry,* New Delhi: Prentice Hall, 1965.

Mukherjee R.K., *West Bengal Family Structures,* 194&.77, MacMillan, 1977.

Murdock G.P., *Social Structure,* New York: Free Press, 1949.

Nandy A., "Need Achievement in a Calcutta Suburb" in Singer M.(ed), *op. cit.*

Oommen R.K., "The Legal Profession in India: Some Sociological Perspectives," *Indian Bar Review,* Vol. X, No.1, 1983.

Oommen T.K., "Insiders and Outsiders in India: Primordial Collectivism and Cultural Pluralism in Nation-Building," *International Sociology,* VII. I (I) March, 1985.

Owens R., "Peasant Entrepreneurs in an Industrial City," in Singer M. (ed.) *op. cit.*

Panikkar K.M., *The Foundations of New India,* London: George Alen and Unwin, 1963.

Patterson M.L.P., "Chitpavan Brahman Family Histories: Sources for a Study of Social Structure and Social Change in Maharashtra" in Singer and Cohn (ed) *Structure and Change in Indian Society,* Chicago: Aldine Publishing Company, 1968.

Rao M.S.A., *Social Movements in India,* Vol. I, New Delhi: Manohar, 1978.

Ross A.D., *Hindu Family in its Urban Settings,* Toronto: University of Toronto Press, 1961.

Rudolph L.I. and Rudolph S.H., *In Pursuit of Laakshmi,* Hyderabad: Orient Longman, 1987.

Saberwal S., *Mobile Men: Limits to Social Change in Urban Punjab,* 1976.

Safa H.I., *Towards a Political Economy of Urbanization in Third World Countries,* Delhi: Oxford University Press, 1982.

Seal Anil, "Imperialism and Nationalism in India" in Gallagher John, Johson Gordon and Seal Anil (ed), *Locality, Province and Nation: Essays on Indian Politics 1870 to 1940,* Cambridge University Press, 1973.

Shoji Ito, "A Note on the Business Combines in India with Special Reference to the Nattu Kottai Chettiers," The *Developing Economics,* Vol. IV, No.3, 1966.

Singer M., "Indian Joint Family in Modern Industry" in Singer and Cohn (ed) *op. cit.,*

When a Great Tradition Modernizes: An Anthropological Approach to Indian Civilization, New York: Praeger Publishers, 1972.

Singh K.S., "From Ethnicity to Regionalism: A Study in Tribal Politics and Movements in Chotanagpur from 1900 to 1975" in Malik S.C., *Dissent, Protest and Reform in Indian Civilization,* Simla: IIAS, 1977.

Singh Yogendra, "Indian Sociology," *Current Sociology,* Vol. 34, No.2, 1986.

Indian Sociology: Social Conditioning and Emerging Concerns, New Delhi: Vistar-Sage Publications, 1987.

"Legal System, Legitimation and Social Change" in Pillai S.D. (ed), *Aspects of Changing India,* Bombay: Popular Prakashan, 1976.

Modernization of Indian Tradition, New Delhi: Thompson Press, 1973.

"Relevant Sociology (1)," *Relevant Sociology: A Journal of Contemporary Sociology,* Vol. I, No. I, 1984.

"The changing Patterns of Social Stratification in India" in Srinivas M.N. et. al. (ed), *Dimensions of Social Change in India,* Allied Publishers, 1977.

Sivakumar S.S., "Family Size, Consumption Expenditure, Income and Land Holdings in an Agrarian Economy: A Critique of Some Populist Notions," *Economic and Political Weekly,* Vol. XI, No. 30, 1976.

Spodek H., "The Manchesterisation of Ahmedabad," *Economic Weekly,* Vol. XVII, 1965.

Stokes Eric, *The English Utilitarians and India,* Oxford University Press, 1959.

Sujata K., "Dynamics of the Family Firm in India: An Exploratory Analysis of the Role of Family and Kinship in Industrial Entrepreneurship," M.Phil. Dissertation, Jawaharlal Nehru University, New Delhi: 1982.

The Economist, May 4, 1991.

The Economist, November 16,1991

Thompson E.P., *The Making of the English Working Class,* London: Penguin Press, 1968.

The Poverty of Theory and Other Essays, London: Marlin Press, 1979. Timberg, T.A., *The Marwaris: From Traders to Industrialists,* New Delhi: Vikas Publishing House, 1978.

Weiner Myron, *Sons of the Soil;* Delhi: Oxford University Press, 1978.

Zeldin Theodore, *France 1848-1945: Intellect and Pride,* New York: Oxford University Press, 1980.

France 1848-1945: *Politics and Anger,* New York: Oxford University Press, 1979.

Index